ACRL Publications in Librarianship no. 37

The role of the beginning librarian in university libraries

RALPH M. EDWARDS

American Library Association

Chicago 1975

ACRL Publications in Librarianship

LIBRARY OF CONGRESS CATALOGING IN PUBLICATION DATA
Edwards, Ralph M

The role of the beginning librarian in university
libraries.

(ACRL publications in librarianship; no. 37)
Bibliography: p.
1. College librarians. 2. Library science—
Philosophy. 3. Libraries, University and college—
California. I. Title. II. Series: Association of
College and Research Libraries. ACRL publications in
librarianship; no. 37.
Z674.A75 no. 37 [Z675.U5]   020'.1   75-30693
ISBN 0-8389-3167-7

Printed in the United States of America

Contents

Tables

Introduction

In a discussion of the basic issues of librarianship, Conrad Rawski recently raised a question about "what librarians do when they are doing well as librarians."[1] This book is an attempt to explore some answers to that question, especially as those answers relate to university librarians and, more specifically, to beginning librarians in university libraries. It describes a study of the roles and performance of the beginning librarians in the University of California libraries, and it attempts to fit the report of that study into a larger historical and theoretical perspective that will be informative for all university librarians and, it is hoped, for librarians in other types of libraries as well.

Librarianship, as the profession that has assumed the responsibility for collecting, organizing, and facilitating the use of recorded knowledge and ideas, should, it would seem, be in a very strong position in a world that is producing information at a constantly accelerating rate and that must depend more and more on effective use of this information. The complex nature of modern human societies and activities would lead one to expect librarians, the handlers of recorded information, to be among the most highly valued professionals. And yet it is quite obvious that this is not so.

This book was shaped by the belief that one of the primary reasons for the low status of librarianship is that it has failed to examine and define carefully enough and critically enough for its own understanding the role that it is playing and the role that it *might* play. Librarians, on the whole, do not know what librarians do when they are doing well as librarians, and much less do they understand what constitutes excellence in professional library service.

The more I work in librarianship, the more dismayed I become at the vagueness and inconsistencies of the conceptions so many librarians have about their roles. It is a subject to which they seem to give very little attention. And the results of this lack of attention are painfully apparent in the inadequate performance of all too many librarians. The profession—without clear knowledge about what it is trying to do and, of course, without knowledge of how well it is doing it—is falling short of meeting the information needs of society.

In an attempt to make some contribution to filling some of the knowledge gaps, I decided to do my doctoral dissertation on the roles of beginning librarians in the University of California libraries. I hoped that the study could reveal something about what was being done on a day-to-day basis by the librarian in university libraries on his or her first job following acquisition of the professional library degree.

I felt there was also a need to know something about how this beginning librarian conceived of his role and how those with managerial authority in the university library conceived of the beginner's role and the way he was carrying it out.

This book grew out of the dissertation study, and the results of the study are reported in chapters 3 through 6.

The book, however, goes beyond the findings of the University of California study because recent developments in professional thinking on these matters have gone beyond anything found in the study. The conceptual gaps are being closed by a few leading thinkers in librarianship, and it will surely be only a matter of time until this new thinking will have a salutary impact on library practice and on the quality of the services being offered by librarians.

Chapter 2 explores the development of (1) these recent concepts of library professionalism and (2) a new, higher level of library service that could be expected from genuine library professionals. Chapter 7 suggests some implications of these concepts for the role of beginning librarians in university libraries.

Chapter 1

Historical and traditional roles of librarians

The definition of the expected and "proper" role of the academic librarian has apparently been a matter of concern and controversy since the beginning of academic libraries in this country. During the early years of the development of American colleges, their libraries were very small and the librarian was a "library keeper." His collection was little used; his primary duty was to protect and preserve books. But even so, Louis Shores tells us in his study of the libraries of the nine colonial colleges, "a careful study of trustee and faculty minutes reveals surprisingly great attention paid to the librarian's problems in administering the college's book resources. Vote after vote recorded by presidents and professors shows how even in those early days the librarian's function was considered of college-wide import."[1]

The conclusion most frequently arrived at in these deliberations and votes was that the librarian's primary function was to protect the books and exercise control over their use. Books were rare and expensive. Publishing in the colonies was of little significance; most of the books in the college collections had to come from England. College budgets were very small, and gifts had to be depended upon for additions to the collections or replacements for lost or destroyed volumes.

An example of the seriousness in which the librarian's responsibility to protect the books was held is the vote in 1707 by the Harvard Corporation, that

> the Library-keeper within the Space of one month next coming, take an inventory, of all Books, mathematicall instruments, & other things of value

committed to his Custody, & Give receipt for them to the President, to be accompted for by him at the Expiration of his year annually, or at his leaving his place, before he receive his salary.[2]

When Mr. Harpur, "the Mathematical Teacher in the College," was appointed librarian at Columbia in 1763, it was ordered that

the said Mr. Harpur make a Catalogue of the Books that now are and hereafter may belong to the Library and deliver a Copy thereof to the President of the College and another Copy to the Clerk of this Corporation, and also that he be accountable for the said Books.[3]

Shores' book, the most thorough and comprehensive history of the early American college libraries, shows that there were very capable and dedicated men—a few of them among the leading men of their time—who were willing to accept the responsibilities of librarians. But Shores also makes it quite clear that those who appointed them saw the librarian's function as primarily that of guarding the books. The college records indicate that the function of adding to or improving the collections was of less concern to the governing boards than the function of preserving those collections, and certainly the function of the librarian as one who promotes the use of the library's collection, or even as one who attempts to make the collection easier to use, was not recognized by early college officials.

Kenneth Brough's history of the university libraries of Chicago, Columbia, Harvard, and Yale bears out this impression about the function of the librarian as perceived by authorities in the early colleges. Brough points out that throughout the colonial period "books were few and precious, and in the thoughts of college authorities their safekeeping rose in importance far above any desire to make them immediately useful."[4] But Brough's evidence indicates that ideas about what the library should be, and, correspondingly, conceptions about what the librarians should be doing, began to change and to grow in the nineteenth century.

Awareness of some of the inadequacies of the American college libraries appeared early in the 1800s, when young scholars such as George Ticknor and Joseph Green Cogswell discovered the much superior library at Göttingen.[5] When these men returned to America, they brought with them new ideas about the importance of the library to scholarship and the determination to improve American libraries. By the middle of the nineteenth century, Brough points out, Harvard, Yale, and a few other institutions had given their libraries a place of some importance. But he further shows that the great majority of mid-nineteenth-century colleges still had libraries (and librarians) that played no vital part in the educational program.[6]

Additional perspective on what was perceived as the role and function of the librarian is given by Carl M. White. In his *Origins of the American Library School* he described two views of the librarian that were commonly held during the nineteenth century and earlier. One was of the librarian as book lover. Most of the men who figured prominently in the early library history of Europe were distinguished bookmen. The second traditional view was of the librarian as gentleman and scholar.[7] This second view was, of course, not incompatible with the first, but it implied that librarianship was a secondary interest—a "side job" for one whose primary interests lay in some other area of endeavor—and was also indicative of the fact that in most of the world there was no recognition of librarianship as a profession, or even an occupation, in and of itself.

The literature of the last third of the nineteenth century is of particular interest to a study of the roles of librarians because that was the period during which a conception of library professionalism came into existence. After the upheaval of the Civil War, America redirected many of its efforts and energies in a period of rapid building and almost incredible growth. It was also a period of new ideas and daring experimentation.

The fact that more money was available and that books were easier to come by, at least in the leading colleges, made it possible for educators to think about new and better ways of taking advantage of the library in the educational process. As early as 1866, a committee reporting to the Harvard Board of Overseers stated the following in its recommendations:

> The usefulness of books largely depends upon facility of access and the convenience attending them. A building which is merely a place for their deposit and safe keeping has no claim to be called a library; and, unless it be amply provided and furnished with every convenience for their use, the most valuable works are sleeping, and are not living teachers of men.[8]

This role of the library, and consequently of the librarian, is in striking contrast to the role implied by the previously quoted regulations voted at Harvard and Columbia during the preceding century. This was only one of the first indications that during the last third of the nineteenth century the emphasis on the librarian's duties in the leading colleges began turning from restriction and preservation to facilitation and even to promotion of use.

The new emphasis appeared clearly in the writings about academic libraries in the 1876 survey of American libraries by the U.S. Bureau of Education[9] and in the early professional writings of such library leaders

as Justin Winsor and Melvil Dewey. Professor Otis H. Robinson was the
spokesman for college libraries in the 1876 report, and he felt that the
leading question was "How shall the library become the most perfect
educational apparatus?" His answer was that "the chief end [of the
library] is its use,"[10] and the librarian's chief function is to serve as
teacher and guide to libraries, books, and reading. "A librarian," said
Robinson, "should be much more than a keeper of books; he should be
an educator."[11]

Justin Winsor, librarian at Harvard and a leader, along with Melvil
Dewey, in the founding of the American Library Association, repeatedly
stressed (in his reports to the university president) his belief in the
importance of the use of books and in his making them as easy as
possible to use. "It is with me a fundamental principle that books should
be used to the largest extent possible and with the least trouble," he
stated in 1879.[12] Winsor, throughout his tenure, was eager to attract
more students to the library and was pleased when he was able to
multiply the number of books lent.

The beliefs of Melvil Dewey about the function of the librarian were
probably more influential than those of any other man of his time.
Dewey was the first editor of the *American Library Journal,* the first
journal of the library profession in the country, and he was the founder,
at Columbia College, of the first school for training librarians. Furthermore, Dewey was very energetic, even aggressive, in expounding and
promoting his ideas and beliefs.

A statement of these beliefs, as pertains to librarians and their
functions in libraries, appeared in the first issue of the *American Library
Journal.* He contended that

> from the first, libraries have commanded great respect, and much has been
> written of their priceless worth; but the opinion has been largely prevalent
> that a librarian was a keeper only, and had done his full duty if he
> preserved the books from loss, and to a reasonable extent from the worms
> . . . It is not now enough that the books are cared for properly, are well
> arranged, are never lost. It is not enough if the librarian can readily
> produce any book asked for. It is not enough that he can, when asked, give
> advice as to the best books in his collection on any given subject. All these
> things are indispensable, but all these are not enough for our ideal. He
> must see that his library contains, as far as possible, the best books on the
> best subjects, regarding carefully the wants of his special community. Then,
> having the best books, he must create among his people, his pupils, a desire
> to read those books. He must put every facility in the way of readers, so
> that they shall be led on from good to better. He must teach them how,
> after studying their own wants, they may themselves select their reading
> wisely.[13]

Dewey's views about the functions of the librarian were crucial because he exerted so much influence on the programs and goals of education for librarianship during its formative period. The fact that most members of the profession were unable or unwilling to go as far as Dewey urged in the above passage, and the fact that many of them are still unable or unwilling, do not, in themselves, indicate that he lacked influence. Had it not been for Dewey's visionary leanings and his vigor in expounding his ideas, it is probable that the profession would have moved even more slowly. Dewey set an ideal early in the history of library professionalism, and although few librarians have lived up to it even today, there have been a few leaders who have been aware of it and have accepted it as the ideal of librarianship since the time Dewey advocated it.

The leaders of the American Library Association were far from unanimous, however, in their support of formal education as the best means of preparing librarians, and even several of those who supported the establishment of a library school seem to have been concerned largely with teaching the "methods" of library work.[14] Since the arguments centered on whether the better way to prepare librarians was through "training" in a library school or on-the-job apprenticeship, the conception of what the librarian was to be prepared to do would appear to be performance of a quite routine and intellectually undemanding job.

Dewey, despite his often quoted statement of 1884 that "the aim of the School is wholly practical," seems to have had a broader conception of what his school would attempt to accomplish. Sarah Vann, in her study of early training for librarianship, concludes that although his approach was pragmatic, Dewey's goal was to provide the student with the "ability to have a successful career in the library profession," and his conception of such success was an encompassing one.[15]

In an article in 1886, Dewey distinguished between library employment and the library profession,[16] and it was for the latter that he felt his school should provide preparation. But other librarians were not ready at that time (or for many more years) to recognize such distinctions in the various aspects of library work, and Dewey, bowing to necessity, did not pursue and develop the idea in his subsequent writings. His school had to tailor its offerings to the kind of practical training in routine methods of library work that librarians and the employers of librarians wanted from it. Dewey had both vision and idealism, but his pragmatism seems to have been his dominant characteristic after all.

"None of Dewey's contemporaries," says Carl White, "read the meaning of changing library personnel requirements as clearly as he." And the requirement that Dewey saw in the libraries of America was technical training. What was wanted was people who had practical knowledge and skill to establish and operate libraries, and Dewey set up his school as "a systematic apprenticeship" to meet this demand.[17]

The curriculum emphasized, from the beginning, such matters as "attainment of the library hand, accession-book, writing of catalogue cards . . . classification . . . cyclostyling, Hammond typewriter . . . apprenticeship training"—but, even so, it was sharply criticized from without for being theoretical rather than entirely practical.[18]

Other training programs for librarianship were started in various parts of the country during the last decade of the nineteenth century and the first two decades of the twentieth century. They, too, emphasized the practical and the routine and took little cognizance of the higher intellectual aspects of library work. Howard Winger succinctly identified the weakness of these—and many subsequent—library education programs with the following statement:

> Designed to supply dogmatic guidelines for people who lacked thorough scholarly preparation, library school curriculums were too filled with techniques and routines to qualify as professional education.[19]

And although Sara Vann concludes that this was "a period of inquiry concerning the essentials of a program of library training" and a period of experimentation and searching for standards,[20] there is no evidence that substantial progress was made toward defining what a genuinely professional librarianship consists of and how to prepare for it.

In 1919 the Carnegie Corporation of New York commissioned Charles C. Williamson to study and prepare a report on training for library service. Williamson's study, published in 1923, raised, and for the first time discussed at length, the issue of a professional versus a technical definition of the functions of librarians. In the report, he criticized both library administrators and library schools for failing to make clear the qualifications needed for different types of work in libraries and for failing to define the nature and demands of genuinely professional work.

Yet, in spite of devoting the complete first chapter of his book to the failure of the profession to define its functions and distinguish them from the clerical and mechanical functions of library work, Williamson, too, failed to define the professional function of librarians. He stressed that a good, general college education is necessary as a preparation for professional work, and he gave negative definitions, such as "professional tasks—tasks which workers with less adequate general and technical equipment cannot perform without permanent damage to library service,"[21] but he did not clearly define, or give specific examples of, his conception of professional tasks in libraries.

Nor did Williamson's findings and conclusions about the inadequacies of library school programs seem to have much immediate impact on those programs, on practices in libraries, or on the literature of the profession. Fewer than half a dozen articles about the report were listed in *Library Literature* for the period 1921 to 1932, and these articles discussed the report only briefly.

Where the Williamson report made its influence felt was on the future development of education for librarianship. One direct result of the report was the allocation of Carnegie Corporation funds to strengthen library education. Furthermore, according to Louis R. Wilson, the report was widely discussed, and "as a result in part of the preceding studies and discussions by the American Library Association of certification and training, many of the recommendations were carried out later at Columbia, under Dr. Williamson's direction, and at many other library schools."[22]

But the influence of the Williamson report on defining the library profession appears to have been slight. There is no evidence in the literature that the report had any direct influence on the way librarians and library administrators defined and organized the various tasks and positions in their libraries.

The first reported attempt to classify the work done in libraries according to whether it should be done by professional or by clerical staff was a study by Susan Grey Akers of activities performed in cataloging departments. As part of the work leading to her doctoral dissertation at the University of Chicago in 1932, Miss Akers looked at the activities in the cataloging departments of sixty-nine libraries. These libraries represented the various sections of the United States, different-size libraries, and different types of libraries, including high school, college, university, and public libraries. After compiling a list of 190 activities performed in cataloging departments, Miss Akers asked eighty-three catalog librarians from the sixty-nine libraries whether each of these activities was carried on in their cataloging departments; if so, whether it was performed by a professional or a clerical staff member; and whether, in the librarian's opinion, it should be performed by a professional. Her findings were reported in a *Library Quarterly* article in 1935.[23]

The opinions about what work *should* be done by professionals closely matched the reports of what *was* being done by professionals; but the work that professionals were doing in the different libraries showed considerable variation. Thirty-five of the 190 activities were reported performed by professionals by all eighty-three catalog librarians, but only one of the 190 activities was reported performed only by clerical personnel in all cases. There was 90 percent or better agreement among the 83 librarians on whether an activity was professional or clerical in only 87 of the 190 activities, and there were 23 activities about which not even two-thirds of the librarians could agree.

Thus the study indicated wide variations between libraries in the allocation of cataloging department tasks between professional and nonprofessional staffs, and it indicated wide variations between the opinions of librarians as to what should be done by professionals and what should be done by nonprofessionals. But it also indicated considerable satisfaction by the librarians with the way things were being done in their libraries and little interest in reaching a clearer and more widely shared definition of which tasks should be done by professionals and which should be done by clericals. This satisfaction was further indicated by the fact that Miss Akers' study seems not to have been followed by further attempts to define the activities she identified or by studies of activities in other library departments.

During the decade of the 1940s there was evidence of a new interest in task analysis and job classification, stimulated by forces outside librarianship. A shortage of personnel during World War II and development of new concepts of personnel management in other fields seem to have led the library profession to seek a better understanding of the work it was attempting to do and ways to make more effective use of personnel in libraries.

In 1941 the California Library Association published a list of library tasks classified according to whether a task should be performed by a professional or by a nonprofessional. A similar list of tasks had formed part of a 1932 report on professional versus nonprofessional positions in libraries put out by the Certification Committee of the California Library Association. This early list had been reproduced only in mimeograph form but had been in such demand that it was revised in more permanent form in the September 1941 *Bulletin* of the Association.[24]

The article enumerated 176 tasks that it recommended be performed in libraries by professionals and 115 tasks that should be performed by nonprofessionals. According to the article,

> The primary purpose of the classification is to furnish a check list in determining what duties can and should be combined for professional and nonprofessional positions. Although the difficulties which lie in the way of completely separating professional and nonprofessional tasks in a library

are recognized, it is apparent that there is far more confusion between the two types of work than is necessary. The desirability of using nonprofessional workers for routine and clerical work in a library may seem obvious, but the advantages for an effective library organization are enumerated here as a logical preliminary to the classification of tasks which follows:

It is one of the most effective economies by means of which libraries can handle rapidly increasing business with inadequate appropriations.

It tends to raise the standard of professional library service by allowing professional members of the staff more time for work with books and people and for the types of library work which are technical and educational in character.

It makes it possible with the same salary budget to pay better salaries to professional members of the library staff.

The list is useful also in a job analysis—one of the best means by which a library or a group of libraries may establish standards of performance.[25]

In 1948 an American Library Association committee, chaired by Mrs. Theodora R. Brewitt, one of the California Library Association committee members who were responsible for the 1941 list of classified duties, produced for national distribution a similar list of professional and nonprofessional duties in libraries.[26] A new classified task list, published by ALA in 1974, has expanded upon the earlier lists and constitutes a refinement based upon extensive analysis and the rationale of the "systems approach."[27] This new list divides library tasks into three categories: professional, technical, and clerical; and many of the tasks in the professional category in the 1948 list have been placed in the technical or even the clerical category in the 1974 list. Appendix B of this book compares the categorizing of selected library tasks by the two lists.

Another type of publication that appeared frequently in the literature of the 1940s and continued to appear into the 1950s was the job description and classification plan. The most comprehensive and detailed of these plans for the library profession was produced in a series of publications issued in the early 1940s by the American Library Association's Board on Personnel Administration. The plan most relevant to the present study was volume 3 (subtitled "Universities") of *Classification and Pay Plans for Libraries in Institutions of Higher Education.*[28] In this volume the Board attempted to define and explicitly describe every type and class of job in the operations of a university library, to give examples of the typical tasks that should be assigned a person holding that job, to state the minimum qualifications needed by anyone who hoped to perform the job satisfactorily, and to give some indication of how each job should relate to all other jobs in the library in terms of the difficulty of the tasks, the qualifications needed, and the salary to be paid the holder of the job.

Many classification levels were established for both professional and nonprofessional jobs by this 1943 publication: five for nonprofessional jobs and ten for professional jobs. It recognized the necessity of providing for a wide variety of institution types and sizes, even though it limited itself to a description and classification of the jobs in university libraries (as distinguished from degree-conferring four-year institutions and non-degree-conferring institutions of higher education). But even when it is recognized that the classification scheme attempted to provide for several sizes of libraries, ten is a surprisingly large number of levels of professional work. It is difficult to know, more than thirty years later, whether the classifications and job descriptions in these "plans" represented the approved practices of the leading libraries of the day or whether they represented the conceptions of the Board's members about how things ought to be. But it can be said that the definitions of the lowest two levels, and even, in some cases, the third level of professional work, as presented by these 1943 publications, involved a good deal of work now widely considered by librarians as less than professional.

Some tasks, for example, that were listed as typical for professional grade two are "[in the catalog department] adapting L.C. or other cards; keeping shelf list; typing, revising and filing cards; supervising or handling processing details; ... [in the circulation department] handling overdues, handling correspondence; ... revising the work of stack clerks; charging and discharging books at the stack desk."[29] Many more examples of low-level task demands that were assigned to professional positions by the 1943 *Classification and Pay Plans for Libraries in Institutions of Higher Education* could be cited, but the example above should suffice to show that attitudes have changed since that time. It should be noted, however, that the findings of the study of the University of California libraries (described herein in chapter 3) indicate that practices have changed less than attitudes.

Further evidence that personnel administration was a major new concern of the library profession was that it was made the subject of the tenth annual Institute of the University of Chicago's Graduate Library School in 1945. The Institute's introductory paper delivered by J. Donald Kingsley, defined personnel administration as "directly concerned with the development of human powers within a particular organization. It is concerned, therefore, with those methods of adjusting the work force to the work environment and the work environment to the work force which will maximize the creative participation of the individual involved in the common endeavor."[30]

Given this ideal as a goal, it was assumed that

> it is necessary to know in detail what specific operations are combined to form the content of every position on the staff, how each job related to every other job, and what the normal lines of authority and promotion are. Such organizational and job analysis is the foundation upon which depend all other personnel processes. It is an obvious prerequisite to the development of job specifications and the determination of qualifications necessary in recruits. It is the necessary basis for the discovery and charting of lines of promotion. It provides the only equitable basis for salary determination and administration. It facilitates the discovery and elimination of blind-alley positions. Job analysis and classification are, in fact, the starting-points for any modern personnel system.[31]

This, then, was the rationale and justification for the concern with job analysis and position classification that so frequently appeared in the literature of the 1940s and early 1950s.

This concern did not, however, prove effective in defining the "professional" role of the librarian. The job descriptions and classification schemes tended to be limited to descriptions of the jobs as they existed and to classifications based upon logical arrangements of these jobs, but they accepted—and did not consider the reasons for—the broad classification of library employees into the two categories of professional and nonprofessional. Essentially, they accepted the previously established overall classification system in library work as given, and then they systematized and refined it into something more structured and rational than it had been before.

This, no doubt, enabled the library administrator to operate more effectively, and must have proved a useful tool for helping to meet the pressures of rapid growth and expanding concern in higher education that marked the post-World War II years. But for all its concern with better organization and newer methods of personnel administration, the literature of the period does not reveal any serious or penetrating questioning of the basic structures of library organization or the functions and roles of those who had claimed the title of professional in libraries.

The American Library Association for many years sent forms to libraries for reporting library statistics to the Association. During the 1940s these forms defined library professional employees as persons

> performing work of a professional grade which requires training and skill in the theoretical or scientific parts of library work as distinct from its merely mechanical parts. . . . A professional position . . . requires the following educational background: (a) At least a bachelor's degree which includes one year of professional library education in the four years which lead to the bachelor's degree; or (b) An informal education considered by the

librarian as the real equivalent of four years of college work, plus five years' experience in a library of recognized professional standing.[32]

This definition is interesting and revealing in its emphases. The professional is defined two ways: (1) according to the demands of the work he performs and (2) according to the formal education, or formal education combined with working experience, that he has had. The emphasis is clearly on the formal definition of education and work experience rather than on the functional definition of the nature and demands of the work.

Furthermore, the functional definition of professional work as that at a "grade which requires training and skill in the theoretical or scientific parts of library work as distinct from its merely mechanical parts" is not very enlightening. Librarians were widely criticized then, as they are today, for failing to distinguish between professional and nonprofessional work and for failing to limit themselves to performing the former, but it is conceivable that many of them might have found it quite difficult to make the distinction as long as they had only the professional association's definition to serve them as a guide.

ALA's 1948 *Descriptive List of Professional and Non-Professional Duties in Libraries* was, of course, one attempt to provide a much more specific delineation of what constitutes professional and nonprofessional work, but it still lacked clear definitions and a rationale to show the bases for the distinctions that were made between professional and nonprofessional tasks.

The problem was basically the same one J. Periam Danton recognized in 1934[33]: the library profession lacked an adequate philosophical conception of its purposes, role, and goals. Until it had a much clearer idea of what it was trying to accomplish and where it should be going, librarianship could not decide what it should be doing at any one time. A practical result of this confusion was pointed out by Edwin Williams in his 1945 article "Who Does What: Unprofessional Personnel Policies." He concluded that probably not much more than 30 percent of the work in a university library could justifiably be defined as professional. (Findings of the present study indicate that a lower figure may now be considered appropriate.) But most of the university libraries he surveyed had a staff composed of considerably more than 30 percent professionals. Some had well over 50 percent professionals in their total staff.[34]

Wilson and Tauber, in the 1945 edition of *The University Library,* reported even more striking figures on the "heaviness" of professionals in the balance of university library staffs. They found the median for fifty American university libraries to be 66.6 percent of the staff in the professional classification. The high figure for these fifty university libraries was 95.3 percent professional; the lowest figure reported was 30.5 percent.[35] It should be noted, however, that these figures are not an accurate reflection of the total staff situation in the reporting libraries because part-time student help was omitted from the calculations.

Edwin Williams concluded, from his and Wilson and Tauber's findings, that professionals must spend a substantial portion of their time—"at least half of their time in some libraries"[36]—doing nonprofessional work. He criticized this situation for two reasons. He felt that it led to a lowering of professional standards in recruiting new librarians—"it would seem difficult for librarianship to attract and hold desirable recruits if it were not making use of their abilities"—and he recognized that professionals in academic libraries in the United States were not doing as much professional work as should be done. For the first time in American library literature, Williams specifically recognized, and stated in this article, that one reason why librarians should not do clerical work was that not enough time was spent on certain kinds of professional work:

> It is doubtful that there is or will be, in the near future, a real surplus of professional skills. Few libraries are now doing all the reference work they would like to do, or giving as much attention as could profitably be given to building up the collection or improving the catalog. Much more professional work could be undertaken if trained librarians were relieved of clerical duties.[37]

Williams did not develop this argument in his article, nor was it pursued by other writers until much later. The emphasis of those who opposed the assignment of clerical and technical work to professionals was almost always on economic arguments. It is uneconomic to have professionals spend their time performing work that less expensive clerical and paraprofessionals could successfully do. And professionals could not hope substantially to improve their salary position as long as they spent their time performing work that could be done by people who could be obtained at clerical wages.

These were the usual arguments advanced during the 1940s for reorganizing library work to avoid having professionals perform subprofessional work, and they continued to be the most frequently encountered arguments through the 1950s and 1960s insofar as academic libraries were concerned. The recent form these arguments have taken is that the other members of the academic community will not be willing to recognize librarians as academic professionals in status and financial remuneration if librarians continue to spend a substantial portion of their time performing subprofessional work. The literature of academic librarianship still gives little attention to the issue Williams raised of professional functions that are not performed under our present system of work allocation.

The period following World War II was also marked by renewed soul searching and criticism directed toward library education. By this time thirty-two American library schools were accredited by the American Library Association, and all were associated with institutions of higher education. The issues and criticisms surrounding the programs of library education were summarized and discussed by J. Periam Danton in 1946. It is clear from Danton's paper that, despite the fact that progress had been made toward professional education for librarians since Williamson's report of 1923, the professional stature of this education was still one of the major deficiencies and sources of criticism of the library school programs.

> The library school curriculum, in general, and in spite of much change and improvement since Williamson's report, still too greatly emphasizes mere techniques and banausic matters; conversely, far too little attention is paid to principles and policies, to the strictly professional and intellectual aspects of librarianship, to its philosophical bases, content, and implications. [And,] The schools make little or no distinction in their programs between, on the one hand, those aspects of library work which are largely or entirely mechanical-technical in nature and, on the other hand, those aspects which are unmistakably professional.[38]

A few years later Danton delineated in some detail, in a book entitled *Education for Librarianship*,[39] what he saw as a library school curriculum and program that would provide preparation for professional-level work in libraries. His recommendations were based on what he believed were a few basic components, necessary in the program of every library school and in the preparation of every librarian. These components were derived from what he recognized as "the three fundamentals of librarianship: books and other graphic records; readers; and the organization, means and devices which bring books and readers together."[40] The book emphasized theory and principle and an understanding of purposes and goals rather than techniques, and serves as further definition of what Danton saw as the professional role of the librarian.

Note should be made of Danton's inclusion of the study of "reading needs, interests, [and] habits" of library users as one of the indispensable components of the library school curriculum[41] and his recognition that such study often was not included in library education programs. Thus he, like Edwin Williams, recognized that crucial areas of professional responsibility were inadequately covered. Libraries and library schools were overlooking, or underemphasizing, certain types of professional activities and functions, such as learning more about the interests, habits, and needs of the libraries' clientele.

Finally, to bring this survey of historical and traditional roles of librarians to the early 1950s, it is worthwhile looking at a study reported by Herner and Heatwole. The study concerned itself with the work that was done in a library, in this case a physics library at Johns Hopkins University.[42] Each "job" that library staff members were asked to do was listed, categorized as professional or nonprofessional, and the work of the staff was timed to determine the average number of hours per day needed for performing each job. The following [43] is the analysis of the average daily work load of the professional jobs.

LIBRARY JOBS	TIME REQUIRED PER DAY
ACQUISITION AND PROCESSING	
Selection of new acquisitions	1 hr.
Interlibrary loan-expediting details	4
Selection and revision of basic catalog subject headings and classifying and cataloging of new acquisitions	4
Scheduling purchases and placing orders	3
REFERENCE SERVICES	
Literature analysis (for pertinent articles, book reviews, etc.)	2
Technical reference assistance	3
Arranging for translations	$\frac{1}{4}$
Compilation and editing of bibliographies	$\frac{1}{4}$
Editing of *Weekly Bulletin*	$\frac{1}{2}$
LIBRARY ADMINISTRATION	
Reports, planning, supervision and training of staff, attendance at staff and professional meetings, visits to other libraries, etc.	4

The total man-hours required for professional duties in this university physics library were thus determined to be 22 per day, and when this total was divided by 6.8 (the number of hours in the average work day), it was found that at least three full-time professional staff members were needed to perform the professional work of the library.

Herner and Heatwole's most interesting findings, from the point of view of the present study, were those about the priorities assigned the various tasks defined as professional, as revealed by the amount of time spent on each of the tasks. It is obvious that the professional function of the selection of materials for the library was not given as much time (one hour) as the professional function of organizing and cataloging the materials (four hours), or even as much time as the professionally questionable tasks of scheduling purchases and placing orders (three hours).

Time spent working with the library users for the purpose of determining and analyzing their library needs did not receive recognition as a separate category of work in the above analysis of work load. This fact is perhaps indicative of the priority assigned this professional function. However, it is stated in a subsequent job classification that *part* of the administrative function consists of attending "technical meetings within the organization in order to keep informed of technical plans and help implement them with adequate published materials" and making "visits to members of the scientific and technical staffs to apprise himself [the head librarian] of their individual bibliographic needs."[44] Only one of the three professional staff members was shown as making such visits to the library users. It could perhaps be assumed that some informal study of the library needs of the people this library was intended to serve was also being carried out under "technical reference assistance." But this category, which must have included all the typical reference work of helping individuals find answers to specific questions, averaged three hours per day—one hour less than was devoted to the details of expediting interlibrary loans.

No other work and time allocation studies, comparable to that of Herner and Heatwole, have been reported in the literature about academic libraries. It is therefore impossible to conclude from published evidence that what was found at the Johns Hopkins physics library was, or is, typical of the professional work priorities in other research libraries. But, combined with the findings reported in chapters 3 and 4 of the present study, there is good reason to think that similar priorities exist in universities in other parts of the country and that these priorities may not have changed significantly over a twenty-year period. They might be characterized as the priorities of a well-organized, smoothly functioning, and efficient library operation.

The role of the librarian, during the years looked at in this chapter, underwent gradual evolution from "library keeper" to "library operator." The librarian, as operator in university and research libraries, was and is primarily concerned with the library's internal operations and its functioning as a flow of materials and an organization of people. Some responsibility is accepted for selection of materials in collection building, for bibliographic control through content analysis, indexing and classifying, and for direct aid to clients, but these activities do not seem to command either the interest or the time that operational and managerial activities and problems command.   The attention and time of the librarian as library operator are devoted more to systems for carrying out routine operations, to organizing and supervising personnel, and generally to operational problem solving and keeping the library "shipshape" and running smoothly.

   The focus of interest of both the library keeper and the library operator is on the library itself rather than on the clientele, the people for whom the library exists.

Chapter 2

Library professionalism and newer conceptions of the librarian's role

The importance of the role of the library operator (or library keeper) is not discounted here. It is, of course, essential if library service is to be effective, and it is a role that will probably involve more time of more people in the future than it does now. But by itself it falls short of what is needed. The library operator, just as the library keeper before him, is necessary for the success of the professional service of librarianship, but he is not sufficient in himself.

More is needed; more is possible; more can and should be asked of the library profession.

A newer and more sophisticated conception of the librarian as a professional with a genuinely professional service to offer seems to be gaining ground among certain types of librarians. This chapter will look at the development of that conception and attempt to define and explore the implications of the librarian's role as a professional who provides professional information services.

During the early 1950s new interest in the status of the librarian appeared and there was again an attempt to define and establish the claims of librarianship to professionalism. Robert Leigh, in his study of the public library at the beginning of the decade, took up the question "What is a profession?" He found that

> A profession possesses specialized, communicable techniques based upon:
> (1) prolonged intellectual training; (2) content of training that includes
> generalizations or principles; (3) the application of the principles in

concrete professional practice, a complex process requiring the exercise of disciplined, individual judgment. To put it in another way, the specialized methods acquired in professional training always include something more than rule-of-thumb procedures or routinized skills.[1]

Leigh considered to what extent librarianship met the criteria and shared the common characteristics of a profession, as he had outlined them. His conclusion was that librarians were, at that time, members of a "skilled occupation on the way to becoming a profession."[2] He did not, in the public library study, attempt to define the professional and nonprofessional aspects of the work of librarians. He said, in this connection, that he was unable to find many job classifications and descriptions by which professional positions could be identified. He attributed this primarily to the fact that the small size of many library units made specialization, even into professional and nonprofessional functions, impossible.

The following year Harold Lancour made a much more positive statement in support of the professionalism of librarianship. In an article in *Library Journal* he asserted:

> One of the fundamental assumptions of this paper is that librarianship is a profession. By definition it is also a learned profession for as Abraham Flexner has pointed out there can be no such thing as an unlearned profession. Learning is a synonym for scholarship. Thus, by extension, we can conclude that members of the library profession will have an accurate and wide knowledge of the principles, both in theory and in application, upon which librarianship is based as well as of the materials of which libraries are formed. Further, this knowledge is gained through a period of directed and supervised disciplined study, followed by a never-ending period of observation, experiment, and reflection.

Lancour's emphasis on the scholarly nature of professionalism led him to conclude that the most important aspect of the training for a profession should be the training in research:

> While it is essential that the period of training conveys to the student known facts concerning professional practice and motivating principles, it must also train the student in the methodology of testing, study, and research and the ability to report the results of such study lucidly and intelligibly. Only in this way can we ensure a body of professional workers who have an interest in and a capacity for sound and critical analysis of professional situations and problems.[3]

Lancour concluded his article with a definition of "the discipline of librarianship." He saw three broad and essential aspects to this dis-

cipline: (1) "a knowledge of recorded materials, their content, characteristics, potentialities, uses, and effects on people," (2) "an understanding
of the place of the library in society, why libraries have been established,
what purpose they serve," and (3) "an awareness of the educational
needs of the community of individuals to which any library is responsible, and the way in which these needs may be met." "This," said
Lancour, "is the stuff of librarianship."[4]

Shortly after Lancour's article was published, the same subject was
taken up—in greater depth and with more thorough consideration of the
basic elements of professional scholarship—by Pierce Butler. Butler, too,
concluded that librarianship is inherently a profession, and a high-level
profession. But he also concluded that librarians have not in most cases
been professionals, as he defined the term, because they preferred to
slight intellectual content in favor of techniques, operations, and the
pursuit of fads.

Because his concern was with the basis of professionalism, Butler's
paper did not spell out the aspects of work in libraries that could
logically or practically be classified as professional. And, it should be
added, the implications of what he said would probably lead to the
conclusion that for a librarian who is genuinely professional, such a
spelling out would be unnecessary.

> The activities of a working librarian are of almost infinite variety. The
> world of books in which he operates is of terrifying magnitude. The cultural
> benefits he mediates are nearly as numerous as the individuals he serves.
> The social groups and institutions with which he co-operates are in-
> extricably interrelated and overlapping. And most of the forces to which he
> must respond lie beyond his control. Yet somehow the librarian must
> manage to maintain a sense of direction and perspective amid this chaos of
> thought and activity. He does this in part by devising instruments and
> processes for doing things effectively, economically, and conveniently. He
> does it in part by reducing his experience and problems to objective,
> quantitative, and predictive order. And he does it in part by raising
> sentiment in himself and others to the level of realistic, rational, and
> normative wisdom.[5]

If the librarian has the "specific humanistic perspective" Butler sees as
necessary, and if his "scholarship is truly professional," he will be able to
do these things for himself and to decide for himself what his *professional* tasks are to be.

Ten years after Lancour's and Butler's analyses of the professionalism
of librarianship, the question was taken up again, and considered in
some depth, at the twenty-sixth annual conference of the Graduate
Library School at the University of Chicago. Of particular relevance to

the present study was the discussion of "the knowledge base of the librarian" in the paper by William J. Goode. Goode concluded that

> librarians themselves have found it extremely difficult to define their professional role and the knowledge on which it rests.
>
> . . . In his survey of librarians in the Pacific Northwest, Naegele has commented that there seem to be no clear standards as to how much librarians should know; we must add that this applies as well to *what* the librarian should know. The repeated calls which librarians have made for a "philosophy of librarianship" essentially express the need to define what is the intellectual problem of the occupation. . . . The specific knowledge which a librarian must possess is not clear.[6]

A 1968 book by Dale Eugene Shaffer attempted a thorough and comprehensive definition of "a profession" and wrestled with the term's applicability to librarianship.[7] Shaffer, too, concluded that one of the basic elements of a true profession is a body of knowledge, a set of intellectualized principles: a *science,* to put it in one word. And he also recognized the weakness of librarianship in developing its peculiar body of knowledge or science. Shaffer at one point asks whether librarians, if they are liberated from clerical duties and routines, will be prepared to perform as true professionals.[8] Not only can he not provide a reassuring answer to that question but he is not even able to define satisfactorily what performing as a true professional would mean. He, too, is unable, despite his methodical and extensive analysis, to make clear just what constitutes the body of knowledge that is basic to a profession of librarianship.

An even more discouraging view of the condition of library professionalism was taken in 1968 in an article by Mary Lee Bundy and Paul Wasserman. This article directs sharp criticism toward nearly all the different groups that form librarianship: library educators, library administrators, working librarians, and the students who prepare for work in the field. But the failure of individuals to organize into viable professional groups that exert the power to create situations in which genuinely professional behavior is possible is a central theme of the article. The failure of librarianship to define its goals and purposes in terms of its clients is seen as its chief deficiency. Bundy and Wasserman conclude that

> viewed against the perspective of history, librarianship can be seen to have made only slow and gradual evolution as a profession and exists now as only a marginal entry in the competitive race for professional status. The conditions of modern times, however, are such that if librarianship does not move much more rapidly forward toward enhanced professionalism, the

field will not only decline rapidly, but ultimately face obsolescence. Already, traditional and conventional libraries are being replaced as new agencies and new practitioners respond more appropriately to changing requirements for information and professional service.[9]

The use of "professional" deserves further discussion at this point. It has been used and misused in many different contexts and senses, and it has taken on so much emotional freight as a prestige symbol that it is now surrounded by confusion and is difficult to define for precise and effective use. An approach that provides a different and useful perspective was adopted by Howard M. Vollmer and Donald Mills in their exploration of the subject:

> We avoid the use of the term "professional," except as an "ideal type" of occupational organization which provides the model of the form that would result if any occupational group became completely professionalized. In this way, we wish to avoid discussion of whether or not any particular occupational group is "really a profession," or not. . . . We feel that it is much more fruitful to ask "how professionalized."[10]

The following six essential criteria of such an "ideal type" have been abstracted from the extensive literature on professions and professionalism.

1. A body of knowledge and systematically organized theory underlies and is necessary to the performance of a professional service.[11] It follows from this that the activities involved are essentially intellectual in character and require the application of thought, judgment, and decision making to each problem.

> The execution or application of a thought-out technique—be it crude or exquisite, physical or mental—is after all routine. Some one back of the routineer has done the thinking and therefore bears the responsibility, and he alone deserves to be considered professional.[12]

2. The services offered by a profession are very important to society and, therefore, are a matter of broad public concern.[13]

3. Because of the superior knowledge and competence of the members of a profession, that profession is granted a monopoly on the right to perform its professional service and on the right to choose and admit new members to its ranks.[14]

4. The fact that the professional must possess superior knowledge also means that no one outside the profession can be qualified to exercise authority over, or even to evaluate dependably the quality of, the service of the professional members.[15]

5. Because society grants a monopoly and defers to the authority of a profession, it is incumbent on the members of the profession to establish and adhere to a stringently self-regulating code of ethics in which the good of the society takes precedence over the personal benefit of the members of the profession.[16]

6. The individual member of a profession becomes part of a professional "culture," and he shares its altruistic motivations, accepts his part of its responsibility to society, and takes pride in its accomplishments. His professional role becomes, in the process, a central aspect of his life and self-concept.[17]

Other characteristics of a profession might be added to this list, but these are the essential ones; and most of the others derive from the six listed here. By applying these criteria of an ideal to librarianship, it is possible to delineate a prototypical profession of librarianship against which the actual roles of librarians may be related and interpreted.

Harold Lancour, it will be remembered, succinctly described the knowledge and theory base of a profession of librarianship. He listed its three broad and essential aspects as (1) "a knowledge of recorded materials, their content, characteristics, potentialities, uses, and effects on people," (2) "an understanding of the place of the library in society, why libraries have been established, what purpose they serve [and might potentially serve]," and (3) "an awareness of the educational needs of the community of individuals to which any library is responsible, and the way in which these needs may be met."[18] Implied here, but not often explicit, is that the body of knowledge of any individual librarian will consist in large part of knowledge of a subject discipline.

For example, the librarian who hopes to provide significant library service to advanced students and scholars in psychology at a university must accept advanced and in-depth knowledge of psychology as a necessary component of his professional body of knowledge. This subject knowledge will probably be much the largest component in the total body of knowledge of the successful librarian in the university community.

There is no question that these bodies of knowledge and theory are potentially of enormous scope and are highly demanding intellectually. Librarianship still falls short in recognizing and systematically developing and organizing the knowledge that is relevant to its services. It has been especially lax about investigating and building knowledge and theory about the needs of its clients and how they approach and use recorded information. But few professions—even those that are much more widely recognized and accepted—are based upon bodies of knowledge comparable in breadth of concern and intellectual challenge to those of librarianship.

The service offered to a client by librarianship is access to the information he needs and can effectively use at any particular time. ("Information" is used here in a very broad sense to include everything in a library, i.e., nonprint, artistic, and literary matter as well as the factual and expository writing usually implied by the term.) This service is important to the client (and to society) insofar as it is important (and socially useful) for him to obtain the information he needs or desires. The fact that the service has not been widely recognized as important and has not often been a matter of broad public concern may mean that most of society's needs for information have been satisfactorily met elsewhere, or that society does not value most recorded information very highly, or that librarianship has traditionally done such a poor job of providing the service that society has never discovered how valuable it might be. Perhaps all three of these conditions may be true to varying degree in different places and situations. Society may not even be aware of how much it needs information.

Librarianship has won a monopoly on the right to perform its professional service in most libraries of any size. The right of the profession to choose and educate its members has also been widely recognized and granted. But the authority and superior expertise of the members of the profession in providing their service is not granted willingly by many clients. This problem is aggravated by the fact that a very important part of the professional service should, and often does, take place before the arrival of the client with his need for service. Selection, acquisition, and organization of information in anticipation of its need is a very important part of the professional service but is often taken for granted by the client. But it must be admitted that the reason why university library clients have usually refused to grant professional authority to librarians is that few librarians have mastered a sufficient body of professional knowledge to enable them to deserve that authority. As noted above, the weaknesses of the librarian have typically been in knowledge of the appropriate subject disciplines and of client needs and information use patterns.

If a profession of librarianship were to meet the criteria of the ideal profession, its self-regulating code of ethics would demand that the librarian keep current with the existence and location of information his clients might need and accept responsibility for his own continuing growth and development in his field. The code would also require that the librarian provide the client impartial, unbiased access to all relevant information. The danger of censorship by outside agencies is widely recognized and opposed by librarians; the danger of censorship by members of the profession is, unfortunately, more difficult to recognize and deal with. The professional ethics of librarianship, like that of most other professions, also requires impartiality and willingness to provide the professional service to all who can benefit from it, without regard to academic status, political, religious or social opinions, or racial or ethnic characteristics.

Finally, librarianship must have a clear identity as a profession with which its members can identify and whose values they can accept and internalize. Out of this identity can grow the altruistic motivations and dedication, sense of responsibility, and many rewards of the professional role. A strong professional organization is one of the early steps toward achievement of such an identity.

The above description represents a theoretical ideal, but there is a genuine question whether this ideal is accepted in practice by librarians. What constitutes library professionalism and what are its intellectual foundations were not, in fact, the questions that attracted the interest of librarians in the 1960s. The two themes that dominated the literature of academic library administration during the decade were "manpower utilization" and the status of librarians. Certainly the manpower concerns were related to the questions of professional roles, as were those about the status of librarians in the academic community, but the impetus toward improving the utilization of manpower came more from a perceived shortage of librarians and from a desire to make the most effective use of staff members because of budgetary pressures. The "President's Special Program," which dealt with a central theme at the American Library Association conference in San Francisco in 1967, was titled "Crisis in Library Manpower: Myth and Reality."[19]

What may very likely prove to be the culminating document on the perceived problem of manpower shortage in libraries was the "Library Education and Manpower" policy proposal of Lester Asheim of the Office for Library Education of the American Library Association.[20] This proposal's most important recommendations were that the nonprofessional personnel structure of libraries be expanded, that a "middle level" paraprofessional category of personnel be established and officially recognized, and that the persons in this paraprofessional category (to have the titles Library Associate and Library Technical Assistant) be assigned many of the marginally professional tasks that librarians have been doing in libraries. This policy proposal was accepted and the policy was adopted by the American Library Association at its 1970 convention in Detroit.

The other major theme of the literature of the 1960s was concern with the academic status of the college and university librarian. The issue appeared early in the decade in a 1961 Graduate Library School Conference paper by Harold Lancour.[21] Margit Kraft developed it further in a plea for scholarship and specialization in library education.[22]

Many writings of the latter half of the decade tied the status of the librarian to issues of organization and authority structure in academic libraries. One of the leading advocates of a "collegial" structure in academic libraries is Eldred Smith, whose articles call for an authority structure for carrying out professional library functions that would be quite different from the traditional structures.[23] Smith sees serious obstacles in the way of genuine professionalism and, therefore, of professional status under present practices.

> A crucial problem is the bureaucratic structure of libraries, which emphasized institutional goals and loyalties. Professional service functions must be made clearly primary, and distinguished from nonprofessional, secondary institutional functions. Librarians must transform their hierarchical, bureaucratic junctions with each other into collegial, professional relations.
>
> This means that decision-making in such matters as collection development, bibliographical control, and information service must be within the discretion of the individual expert practitioner, acting within a collegial framework, and restricted only by the most necessary institutional restraints. Supervision of professional activity must be abandoned and replaced by general administrative coordination and peer evaluation. Rewards must be based primarily on professional accomplishment, not bureaucratic position; academic benefits must be substantial enough to attract, keep, and develop top-flight personnel.[24]

California librarians seem to have been leaders in the 1960s of this drive toward restructuring bureaucratic library organization and toward militancy in working for improved status, but similar voices were heard elsewhere as well. Examples are David Wilder of the University of Manitoba and David Kaser of Cornell University.[25] A collection of writings on the status of the academic librarian and the problems in improving it was compiled by Lewis Branscomb and published as *The Case of Faculty Status for Academic Librarians.*[26]

The half decade of the 1970s has seen a dramatic change from the situation of the previous two decades in higher education and in academic libraries. The manpower shortage has been replaced by a job shortage, and the upward spiraling cost of nearly everything has become the pressing problem of the times. Not surprisingly, the interest in manpower utilization and effective organization has continued to grow.

The need to make the best possible use of expensive professional staff time has further stimulated attempts to define a higher level and more productive role for the professional. In many libraries this has resulted in moving the professional staff into higher positions in the staff hierarchy and in a consequent reduction in the proportion of professionals to nonprofessionals in the total organization. But to increase managerial and supervisory responsibilities as a method of treating the cost-effectiveness problem largely ignores the distinctively professional functions of librarianship. The librarian becomes a library manager who supervises the nonprofessional staff members, who become library operators.

This condition only illustrates that practice often lags behind the best thinking. And a few people in librarianship report some very good thinking about the implications of the model of professionalism and the roles the librarian might play as a professional. These writers recognize that the professional expertise of librarianship is urgently needed by society for help in solving the extremely difficult problems of access to needed and appropriate recorded information. The smoothly functioning library, in which routine operations are carried out with efficiency and low cost, is not doing the job that is needed if it is not also giving a great deal of attention to certain professional problems: identifying and understanding the information needs of its clientele; discovering and selecting the most useful and appropriate items of recorded information and knowledge from the incredibly vast bibliographic universe; and finding more effective ways of establishing bibliographic control so that the best information to meet a particular client's needs can be readily retrieved when it is needed.

The distinction between professional and operational functions in libraries was well stated by Neal Harlow in a paper presented at a University of Illinois conference on library education in 1970. According to Harlow,

> a *librarian* must possess a breadth of understanding which will enable him to discover the complex library needs of a mixed community; his primary concern is with the social effects of the institution, what happens outside as a result of actions inside. A *technical worker,* in contrast, must be able to control the apparatus of the library in order to effectively realize its purpose.[27]

G. Edward Evans, in another paper at the same conference, developed the meaning of genuinely professional library functions. He pointed out that "the day of the unsophisticated librarian may well be coming to an end. It can very well be that we need to substitute the specialist, the experts who among other skills 'can step into the collection-development, substantial-reference, and bibliographical-consultant positions that are now largely unfilled.' "[28]

The new conception of the librarian's role that emerged in the late 1960s and early 1970s incorporates the professional body of knowledge and the resultant professional authority into the role of a client-oriented professional who works with a good deal of autonomy and uses the library as a tool in providing professional service to his clientele. This librarian will work largely outside the traditional hierarchical library organization, except as the organization functions as a support to the professional services he offers. He will usually be a specialist whose professional body of knowledge incorporates a subject knowledge in depth, a knowledge of client needs and abilities, and a knowledge of information sources, including intensive knowledge of bibliographic development, bibliographic techniques, and the literature of his specialty. The services offered by this professional will go beyond merely providing bibliographic tools and directions. It will include interpretation of client needs as they relate to information resources, advice and guidance, and recommendations of the best information to meet the client's needs.

These professional services must, of course, be based upon a sound body of subject knowledge and understanding of information use—a body of knowledge and understanding far beyond that of the typical library operator.

Paul Wasserman (rather pessimistically) believes that

> what appears to be emerging and which is yet far from being accepted is a clear shift from institutional identification to client identification . . . [and] the new paradigm contains the basis for a wholly reconstructed sense of the intrinsic professional contribution which departs from prior history and experience. The essential question is whether such experimentation and prototypal development can be expanded, elaborated, and further accommodated within the framework of the library profession and of the field's institutional base. If so, it might well become a new and significant added pattern of response to strengthen the discipline and the institution in order to lend it new vitality and momentum. Or if it is contained and remains exceptional, that coterie of involved individuals may disassociate themselves from the present institutional structure and, like the embryo information science, attempt to forge an emergent professional client-oriented discipline divorced and distinct from librarianship.[29]

It may be too soon to tell whether the role of this new professional will become the central role in librarianship or whether he will even call himself a librarian. As Wasserman suggests, he may be blocked by entrenched organizational structures and forced outside what we call librarianship. Either way, it appears likely that we are seeing a third major phase in the development of the role of the librarian—from librarian as library keeper to librarian as library operator and now to librarian as professional, providing a genuinely professional information service. But this last role is only beginning to emerge. Much remains to be done in defining it and building the knowledge base that will be required to carry it out.

Chapter 3

A study
at the University
of California

The literature surveyed in the previous chapters indicates that even though new ideas are emerging, librarianship has not adequately conceptualized, and does not yet have enough information about, its expected role. Definitions have not been made that can relate theory and ideal to the actual practices in most libraries. Clear and detailed explanations have not been produced that would show librarians what they need to know and need to be able to do in order to function satisfactorily in their roles. This lack of definition and explanation is felt acutely in the professional schools, where decisions must be made daily about the programs of preparation for librarianship; and wise decisions necessarily depend on good information about the role and demands of the profession. No one is likely to be satisfied if students in the library education programs are not prepared for the role they will be expected to play after they have completed their preparation, and yet little is known by library educators about the details of these expected roles and just how they relate to, or how much they depart from, the ideals that the educators and the leaders of the profession might hold.

There is perhaps an even greater obligation to the prospective recruit and the student of librarianship to provide a clear and realistic picture of what will be expected of him as a librarian. He needs to be exposed not only to the ideals of librarianship but to the realities of his prospective career, and especially the realities of the first job, if he is to face that first job without disillusionment and despair on his part and dissatisfaction on the part of his employer.

The decision to study the beginning librarians in the University of California libraries was based upon these beliefs and assumptions. The first purpose of the study was to provide additional information to the library profession about what beginning librarians in university libraries are doing. It was a further intention of the study to show how these practices relate to the ideals about the librarian's role that are held by the beginning librarians, to the ideals held by the senior librarians who guide and supervise beginners, and to the ideals held by library administrators in university libraries. If, in the process, the findings provide useful information for those involved in the education of librarians, the study will have served an additional beneficial purpose. Library educators will, perhaps, be especially interested in the concepts of professionalism and the professional self-identity carried by these beginning librarians into their first job.

Several limitations on the scope of the study were necessary. Attention was focused on beginning librarians, not only because that seemed a logical place to start but because there is a rather pressing need of library schools for more information about what is asked of their graduates after they leave school and enter upon their first job. There is, of course, a need to investigate the tasks performed by librarians at all levels and with all degrees of experience if we are to clarify the professional role of librarianship. There is likewise a need to investigate the conceptions held by librarians about professional roles at all levels of librarianship—the ideals as well as the practices, and their relationship to each other. But because of the limitations of time and resources, the decision was made to confine the study to the roles, ideal and actual, of the beginning librarian in the University of California libraries.

The beginning librarian was defined as a librarian who has worked two years or less (full-time equivalence) in a university library since completing his professional education or first being hired to fill a professional position. The term library administrator refers to those officials who administer and are responsible for the operations of the entire library. This includes the director of the library, his immediate assistants in positions of line authority, and the top personnel officer. The term library supervisor, on the other hand, refers to such middle-management persons as department heads and branch librarians who directly supervise the work of at least one beginning librarian.

"Professional positions" were accepted as such for the study if they were defined as professional by the library. The study did not, however, include positions classified as professional but not as librarian—for example, systems analysts, accountants, and computer programmers.

In most cases the positions within the University of California libraries are clearly distinguishable because the university's budgeting system requires that a position be defined and labeled before money can be made available to pay a person to fill that position. The positions of most of the beginning librarians interviewed are Librarian I, the title applied to the lowest-paid and least demanding professional positions. Preferred practice throughout the University of California system calls for promoting all librarians who are qualified for continued employment to positions at the level of Librarian II after about two years. In some cases beginning librarians are hired to fill positions at a level higher than Librarian I if they possess desired competencies above the minimum requirements.

The terms "work of the librarian" and "job of the librarian" are used interchangeably, and both can be defined as identifiable tasks assigned any position that is classified as a librarian's position. This includes any tasks a librarian has taken on unofficially and on his own initiative.

Preparation for librarianship was defined broadly to include major fields of study at either the graduate or undergraduate level, as well as programs leading to a library science degree and any special knowledge or skills, such as knowledge of a foreign language or computers and their application in libraries. In other words, any academic or technical preparation that librarians consider pertinent to success in filling a particular librarian's position was accepted by this study as coming under the definition of preparation for librarianship.

The university library included the main or general research library of the institution, plus any school, departmental, or branch libraries that are under the same administrative control as the main library and whose personnel are selected by the library administrators. An exception to this definition was made in the case of libraries of the medical and law schools; because of the special nature of the materials with which they work, librarians who held positions in University of California medical and law libraries were excluded from the study.

The study was designed to test two hypotheses, which were originally formulated as follows:

Hypothesis 1:

Beginning librarians in the University of California libraries are asked to perform a wide variety of tasks, many of which are different from the tasks that administrators and supervisors believe they should be prepared to perform. The fact that there are differences between the actual work assignments and the expectations of the positions can be attributed to the following:

1. Library administrators and supervisors believe that beginning librarians do not come to their libraries adequately prepared to do the jobs that are needed in university libraries.

2. The way the work of the library is organized requires beginning librarians to perform subprofessional tasks because much necessary "housekeeping work" would not otherwise be completed.

Hypothesis 2:

Much of the work that is done by persons holding beginning librarian positions is considered less than fully professional by supervisors and by the beginning librarians, but a widely shared and clear conception of the "proper" functions of beginning librarians is not to be found at any level in the university library because neither supervisors nor beginning librarians are able adequately to define the professional functions of university librarianship.   Confusion, vague generalizations, and disagreements are found among librarians at all levels regarding the meaning of library professionalism and the service of the library profession.

To define further the purpose of the study, a few words should perhaps be said about what it did *not* attempt to do. It did not concern itself with the opinions of university librarians about library education programs. The concern was with *what* beginning librarians are expected to know and do in university libraries, not with *how* they should gain this knowledge or *how* they should be prepared to do the work that is needed. These latter concerns were left for other investigations with other approaches and methods.

The libraries of the University of California were chosen for this study because the eight general campuses of the system represent a varied set of institutions, presenting situations in many ways typical of the situations in a wide range of other American universities. They run from the large, long-established, and prestigious Berkeley campus to the new, experimental, and small (but rapidly growing) Santa Cruz campus. And their libraries reflect this variety and diversity.   The eight general campuses are located at Davis, Berkeley, Santa Cruz, Santa Barbara, Los Angeles, Riverside, Irvine, and La Jolla (San Diego). Each campus maintains a general research library as well as satellite departmental or specialized libraries.

The limitation on the number of libraries to be covered made it possible for the investigator to visit each library and study all the positions held by beginning librarians. The investigation was carried out through interviews, through having beginning librarians complete a checklist of the duties they perform, and through analysis of written job descriptions of positions for which beginners could qualify.

The eight directors reported that their libraries employed a total of sixty-one beginning librarians (although two of these did not, it turned out, meet the definition of beginning librarian used in this study) and that these beginners were supervised by forty-seven supervising librarians. The types of work or library to which the sixty-one beginning librarians were assigned are as follows.

Acquisitions	9
Special-subject libraries (biology, Far East, etc.)	9
Special materials collections (rare books, manuscripts, government documents, etc.)	7
Undergraduate libraries	4
Serials	10
Cataloging	11
General reference	11

The interviews were conducted from March through June 1970. Interviews were held with all beginning librarians, with their supervisors, and with the library administrators. The administrators included the university librarian, the personnel officer, and line assistants to the university librarian in cases where these assistants were involved in the organization of professional library positions or in the selection or evaluation of new professional staff members. Twelve administrators were interviewed on the eight campuses: five university librarians, two associate university librarians, three assistant university librarians, and two personnel officers. At least one administrator was interviewed in each of the eight library systems.

After an initial visit to the administrative offices at each library, the next step was to contact each beginning librarian and the supervisors who were to be interviewed. An appointment was made and the librarian was asked to allow at least one hour's time. Each beginning librarian was asked to complete a checklist of library tasks before the interview. A copy of this checklist may be found in Appendix A.

The tasks on the checklist were abstracted from the American Library Association's 1948 *Descriptive List of Professional and Nonprofessional Duties in Libraries.*[1] The sixty tasks on the study's checklist were selected as representative of the wide variety of duties performed regularly in university libraries. They were not expected to cover all the work done by beginning librarians in these libraries but they were intended to include examples of tasks ranging from the simple to the complex and from the clearly nonprofessional to the clearly professional. A few additional tasks that did not appear in the 1948 list, such as "prepare information for automatic data processing" and "develop systems analyses," were added to the checklist in an attempt to make it more up to date. Each beginning librarian was asked to indicate (with a symbol for each of the sixty tasks) whether he performed it frequently as part of his job, or only occasionally, or rarely or never. When the checklist was given to each beginning librarian, a special point was made of the fact that it was a *selected* list of library tasks and that space was provided for the librarian to add any additional tasks that constituted a significant part of the work assigned to his position.

Three different schedules structured the interviewing: one for beginning librarians, one for the supervisors of beginning librarians, and one for library administrators. Copies of these schedules may be found in Appendix C.

One other source of data for this study, in addition to the interviews and the checklist, was four official job descriptions for positions that were not filled by a beginning librarian but could be so filled if one of the positions became vacant.

Conclusions about the value of the findings of a research study must be based upon several considerations, such as the reliability and validity of the data obtained, the number or representativeness of the individuals or items studied, and finally—and perhaps most important—the importance and implications of the questions asked and the hypotheses tested. The interview method of gathering data in an investigation does not always or easily lend itself to statistical or other empirical tests of validity and reliability of results, but certain steps were taken to maximize these factors.

The attempt was made, while formulating the questions, to avoid ambiguity and ill-defined terms (except for "professional," which was purposely undefined in the interviews because it was to bring out information about the way the person being interviewed defined it). The questions, once they were established in the interview schedules, were asked as much as possible in the same way, with the same wording and in the same order. Notes of what was said in answer to interview questions were as full and nearly verbatim as is possible for one who does not write in shorthand. Whenever the person being interviewed asked for definitions of terms or explanation of questions, a conscious effort was made not to influence the direction or content of his subsequent answers. The interviewer at all times attempted to maintain an interested and sympathetic but neutral stance on all issues and in response to all answers and statements.

The person being interviewed was encouraged to express his opinions freely. To facilitate this freedom, it was pointed out to each beginning librarian and supervisor that his name would not appear on the interview notes and that he would not be quoted by name in any written material resulting from the interview. Administrators were told the same, if at any point in the interview they expressed any reservation about putting themselves on record in regard to any topic.

The population covered by the study also deserves discussion. In one sense, the coverage was nearly complete. Fifty-eight of the fifty-nine beginning librarians and forty-five of the forty-seven supervisors in the University of California libraries were interviewed. The twelve top administrators and personnel men represent more than half of those officers. Thus a strong argument can be made for the thoroughness of the investigation as far as the University of California libraries are concerned. But the investigator recognizes and admits that these cannot be said to be statistically representative or even typical of the total population of university libraries in the United States.

The decision to limit the study to the eight library systems of the University of California can be justified, however, by the previously noted fact that there are wide variations and disparities between these libraries and by the fact that they are of considerable interest and importance in and of themselves. They serve institutions that are recognized as leaders in American higher education. They are situated in an area long noted for progressive attitudes and activities in librarianship. And they were for a long time well supported. Libraries such as these can be expected to be in the forefront of library development and activity. For these reasons alone they would be worth studying.

Jobs in American libraries have traditionally been divided into two broad categories: technical services and public services. This division is still applicable in the eight libraries covered by this investigation, but important deviations from the usual conceptions about technical service and public service jobs were apparent in these libraries. Such a deviation was found in serials departments, whose work traditionally consists of acquisitions, record keeping, and cataloging serial publications—or, in other words, technical services. In five of the libraries visited in the study the serials departments maintain a public service desk and provide directional and reference services involving serials. Other examples of the limited applicability of the public services/technical services dichotomy were found in special collections, where the major work of the librarian consists of book selection and reference, but where a substantial amount of ordering and cataloging is also done. As for book selection, it is not at all clear just where it fits into the public services/technical services division, and this is especially so when a faculty plays a part in the book selection activity.

Categorizing the beginning librarians was further complicated by the fact that these positions are occasionally a split assignment between two departments. The librarian, for example, might be assigned half time in the general reference department and half time in the university archives. Three of the positions examined in the study were split assignments between two library departments, and in one of these positions, one of the departments was a technical services department and the other was a public services department.

Despite these deviations and exceptions, the division between technical and public services was employed in the presentation and discussion of the findings because most of the positions in libraries and most of the tasks assigned to them still fit comfortably into one of these categories. The idea that was widely popular in the profession a few years ago, of assigning librarians to subject division libraries and having them do both the reference work and the cataloging of materials for that division, is not applied at any of the libraries covered by this study. Finally, the conceptions about technical and public services continue to hold an important place in education for librarianship and in the minds of students of librarianship when they make plans for their careers.

The fifty-eight beginning librarians who were interviewed and the six additional positions that are not presently filled by a beginning librarian have therefore been categorized for purposes of analysis as follows:

TECHNICAL SERVICES   30
    Acquisitions   9
    Serials   10
    Cataloging   11

PUBLIC SERVICES   34
    Librarians in a branch library specializing in subject matter 9
    Librarians in special collections by type of material (manuscripts,
      government documents, rare books, maps, etc.)   9
    Librarians in undergraduate libraries   4
    Circulation   1
    General reference   11

The average time the fifty-eight beginning librarians had worked in their positions was 13.1 months. Thirty-three of the fifty-eight had had preprofessional experience in libraries. For these thirty-three, the average length of preprofessional work was 1.36 years. Twenty librarians had done their preprofessional work in university libraries and thirteen in school, public, or other libraries. Thirteen of the beginning librarians are male; forty-five are female.

Table 1 is a compilation of the checklist of tasks filled out by beginning librarians. These checklists were obtained for a total of fifty-seven positions. For each task, the number of beginning librarians who reported that they performed that task regularly, occasionally, or never is reported. Tallies are also broken down to show the responses for the twenty-eight technical services librarians and the twenty-nine public services librarians who completed the checklist.

TABLE 1   TASKS PERFORMED BY 57 BEGINNING LIBRARIANS

TASKS	TOTAL (N = 57)			TECHNICAL SERVICES LIBRARIANS (N = 28)			PUBLIC SERVICES LIBRARIANS (N = 29)		
	REGULARLY	OCCASIONALLY	NEVER	REGULARLY	OCCASIONALLY	NEVER	REGULARLY	OCCASIONALLY	NEVER
Train nonprofessional employees	10	28	19	6	13	9	4	15	10
Supervise work of nonprofessional employees	34	13	10	17	5	6	17	8	4
Organize or plan work of others	24	14	19	13	4	11	11	10	8
Participate in library committee meetings	10	23	24	4	8	16	6	15	8
Prepare reports	4	26	27	1	11	16	3	15	11
Dictate letters	5	7	43	4	4	20	1	3	23
Type letters	8	20	29	2	6	20	6	14	8
Read professional literature	24	20	13	11	7	10	13	13	3
Write for professional publication	0	3	54	0	2	26	0	1	28
Attend classes and lectures	5	19	33	2	9	17	3	10	16
Participate in activities of professional organizations	13	21	23	10	10	8	3	11	15
Prepare public relations material	3	12	42	1	2	25	2	10	17
Set up displays	3	11	43	0	1	27	3	10	16
Give tours or lectures	10	16	31	0	5	23	10	11	8

TABLE 1—*Continued*

TASKS	TOTAL (N=57)			TECHNICAL SERVICES LIBRARIANS (N=28)			PUBLIC SERVICES LIBRARIANS (N=29)		
	REGULARLY	OCCASIONALLY	NEVER	REGULARLY	OCCASIONALLY	NEVER	REGULARLY	OCCASIONALLY	NEVER
Read book reviews	19	23	14	8	8	11	11	15	3
Investigate needs of library users	8	14	34	3	2	23	5	12	11
Recommend books for acquisition	17	21	19	6	7	15	11	14	4
Make final decisions on book selection	10	5	42	5	3	20	5	2	22
Check lists of catalogs against library holdings	15	19	23	5	7	16	10	12	7
Look up reviews of books requested by library users	0	15	42	0	2	26	0	13	16
Decide whether or not to duplicate materials	12	15	30	6	7	15	6	8	15
Consider purchase of materials sent on approval	8	7	42	5	3	20	3	4	22
Decide on acceptability of gifts	10	11	36	6	1	21	4	10	15
Arrange exchanges	2	1	54	1	0	27	1	1	27
Select nonbook materials	6	9	42	0	3	25	6	6	17
Order nonbook materials	7	7	43	2	2	24	5	5	19
Examine material for discard or replacement	11	18	27	4	4	20	7	14	7
Interview salesmen	3	3	51	3	1	24	0	2	27
Check orders to see if the books are already in the library	9	15	33	5	4	19	4	11	14
Verify bibliographic information for book orders	14	10	33	7	5	16	7	5	17
Search for difficult trade bibliographic information	7	21	29	5	7	16	2	14	13
Maintain book budget records	1	0	56	1	0	27	0	0	29
Decide where to place book orders	7	2	48	6	1	21	1	1	27
Prepare book orders	9	11	37	5	4	19	4	7	18
Revise book orders	6	5	46	4	3	22	2	2	24
Check incoming books against orders	9	6	41	3	4	22	6	2	19

(Continued)

TABLE 1—*Continued*

TASKS	TOTAL (N=57)			TECHNICAL SERVICES LIBRARIANS (N=28)			PUBLIC SERVICES LIBRARIANS (N=29)		
	REGULARLY	OCCASIONALLY	NEVER	REGULARLY	OCCASIONALLY	NEVER	REGULARLY	OCCASIONALLY	NEVER
File cards, work slips, or other library materials	18	19	20	7	10	11	11	9	9
Revise filing after it has been done by others	10	15	32	5	5	18	5	10	14
Type	26	18	13	11	9	8	15	9	5
Establish or verify cataloging entries	28	9	20	18	7	3	10	2	17
Do descriptive cataloging	21	2	34	13	1	14	8	1	20
Assign classification numbers or reclassify	16	1	40	13	1	14	3	0	26
Assign subject headings	20	5	32	12	1	15	8	4	17
Reconcile L.C. cataloging	19	4	34	13	2	13	6	2	21
Revise cataloging done by someone else	13	6	38	8	2	18	5	4	20
Verify bibliographic information for interlibrary loan	5	11	41	0	1	27	5	10	14
Answer reference questions	29	5	23	1	5	22	28	0	1
Help readers use the catalog	26	12	19	1	9	18	25	3	1
Help readers use reference books	25	5	27	1	2	25	24	3	2
Compile bibliographies for publication	2	4	51	0	2	26	2	2	25
Compile bibliographies for faculty	3	12	42	0	2	26	3	10	16
Work with faculty to help them make better use of library materials in their teaching	3	14	40	0	2	26	3	12	14
Work with faculty on their research projects	3	8	46	0	0	28	3	8	18
Organize and maintain information files	15	9	33	3	2	23	12	7	10
Index	5	5	47	0	0	28	5	5	19
Supervise shelvers	5	4	48	0	0	28	5	4	20
Make decisions about binding	14	9	33	7	4	16	7	5	17
Prepare information for automatic data processing	6	3	47	3	2	23	3	1	24
Develop systems analyses	0	1	55	0	1	27	0	0	28

In addition to the tasks listed on the checklist, thirty-seven others were written in as tasks assigned to their positions and performed regularly by beginning librarians. Most of these additional tasks were mentioned by only one beginning librarian. The tasks are listed below in the wording used by the beginning librarians.

TASKS ADDED TO THE CHECKLIST BY TECHNICAL SERVICES LIBRARIANS

Develop work manual and organize department
Claim serials (added by two librarians)
Take charge of department when department head is absent (added by
    two librarians)
Route incoming materials to other departments (added by two librarians)
Solve "snag" problems in acquisitions
Send form-letter correspondence
Keep records ("statistics") on work performed in the department
Maintenance work on the card catalog
Decide in which collection books belong
Prepare authority cards
Re-catalog books
Work with other librarians in establishing agreeable cataloging practices
Page books from the closed stacks
Make trips to buy books
Ascertain value of books

TASKS ADDED TO THE CHECKLIST BY PUBLIC SERVICES LIBRARIANS

Page books from the closed stacks (added by two librarians)
Teach a class how to use the library
Make analytics (extra cards) for the departmental catalog
Supervise the newspaper collection
Maintain microfilm reading equipment
Route bibliographic information to faculty
Circulation work (check out books or other materials) (added by
    three librarians)
Run serials binding operation (maintain records, see that serials are
    prepared and sent to bindery, supervise assistants)
Catalog portraits
Supervise building guards
Develop self-service reference and use-of-the-library guides
Maintain pamphlet collection budget records
Keep payroll records for department's nonprofessionals
Schedule reference desk coverage
Reshelve reference books (added by two librarians)

Approve and advise on form of theses and dissertations (added
  by two librarians)
Develop pamphlet collection
Maintain looseleaf business service binders
Schedule the work of student assistants
Set up routines for processing foreign and international documents
Shelve books
Help in planning conference
Work on a system for reorganizing the university archives

Only two tasks were checked on the checklist as regularly performed
by half or more of the responding beginning librarians: supervising the
work of nonprofessional employees (regularly performed by thirty-four
of the fifty-seven respondents) and answering reference questions (regularly performed by twenty-nine respondents). Eleven of the tasks were
reported performed regularly by twenty or more respondents:

TASK	REGULARLY PERFORMED
Supervise work of nonprofessional employees	34
Answer reference questions	29
Establish or verify cataloging entries	28
Help readers use the catalog	26
Type	26
Help readers use reference books	25
Organize or plan work of others	24
Read professional literature	24
Physically process books or other materials	23
Do descriptive cataloging	21
Assign subject headings	20

At the opposite extreme, six tasks on the checklist were reported never
or very rarely performed as part of their job by fifty or more of the fifty-
seven respondents:

TASK	RARELY OR NEVER PERFORMED
Write for professional publication	54
Arrange exchanges	54
Interview salesmen	51
Maintain book budget records	56
Develop systems analyses	55
Compile bibliographies for publication	51

Twenty of the sixty tasks on the checklist were assumed by the investigator to be clerical-level tasks or tasks that could be assigned to capable and well-trained nonprofessional library technicians. These twenty tasks were purposely included in the checklist to test the hypothesis that many beginning librarians are still assigned tasks that could be satisfactorily carried out by nonprofessional staff. The twenty tasks that are considered to require less than professional competence and education and the number of beginning librarians who reported performing them regularly or occasionally are shown in Table 2.

TABLE 2   NONPROFESSIONAL TASKS AND THE RATE OF PERFORMANCE (N = 57)

TASK	PERFORMED REGULARLY	PERFORMED OCCASIONALLY
Type	26	18
Physically process books or other materials in any way	23	7
Do descriptive cataloging	21	2
Reconcile L.C. cataloging	19	4
File cards, etc.	18	19
Check lists or catalogs against library holdings	15	19
Verify bibliographic information for book orders	14	10
Revise filing after it has been done by others	10	15
Check order requests to see if books are already in the library	9	15
Prepare book orders	9	11
Check incoming books against orders	9	6
Type letters	8	20
Order nonbook materials	7	7
Revise book orders	6	5
Prepare information for automatic data processing	6	3
Verify bibliographic information for interlibrary loans	5	11
Supervise shelvers	5	4
Set up displays	3	11
Maintain book-budget records	1	0
Look up reviews of books requested by library users	0	15

Admittedly, some of the tasks in Table 2 are intermediate in requirements, between professional and nonprofessional knowledge and competence. Some, such as descriptive cataloging, have traditionally been assigned to professionals, and no doubt a good many professionals would contend that descriptive cataloging is a professional-level task. The investigator feels, however, that descriptive cataloging, verifying bibliographic information for interlibrary loan, and any of the other marginal tasks should be assigned to nonprofessional positions because in most situations they involve the application of established and specific rules. Their successful completion may demand a good deal of knowledge, but they do not often require applications of professional judgment and decision making.

All but four of the fifty-seven beginning librarians reported that they perform at least one of these twenty nonprofessional tasks regularly. And the average number of the nonprofessional tasks reported performed regularly by the different occupational groups of beginning librarians was about four, as shown below:

TYPE OF WORK		AVERAGE PER LIBRARIAN
TECHNICAL SERVICES		3.7
Acquisitions	4.1	
Cataloging	4.0	
Serials	3.1	
PUBLIC SERVICES		4.2
Reference	1.9	
Special materials libraries	5.7	
Special subject libraries	7.0	
Undergraduate libraries	4.5	

The high rates of nonprofessional tasks reported by librarians in special collections and branch libraries are apparently a result of the small size of the staffs in several of these libraries. In some cases there is only one person on duty in the library during much of the time it is open, and that person must necessarily perform all the tasks involved in the ongoing operation of the library. Thus there tends to be a blurring of the distinctions between professional and nonprofessional positions, and persons in both types of position are likely to carry out both professional and nonprofessional tasks. The highest number of nonprofessional tasks performed regularly (fourteen of the twenty listed on the checklist) was reported by a librarian in one of these small, specialized branch libraries.

Chapter 4

The attitudes of librarians toward their roles

A clear pattern of dissatisfaction with the demands, opportunities, and professional level of their jobs emerged from the interviews with the beginning librarians in the University of California libraries.   But a shared conception or definition of what was meant by "professional" in librarianship did not emerge.   Thirty-nine of the fifty-eight beginning librarians were dissatisfied with the professionalism of their jobs. Sixteen felt their jobs were satisfactorily professional in nature, and in three cases the point of view could not be determined.   A typical comment by one of these last three was "I really can't say because I have never understood what is meant by this word professional."

Only a minority felt that their jobs failed to take advantage of their preparation.   The following shows their responses:

	JOB FAILS TO TAKE ADVANTAGE OF PREPARATION	JOB TAKES ADVANTAGE OF PREPARATION (OR NO COMMENT)
Technical services librarians	13	16
Public services librarians	8	21
Total	21	37

One of the surprising things about the responses was that so few of the librarians seemed to have given them previous thought.   In most cases the librarian would ponder the question and then answer "No, I can't think of any" or "No, I don't think so."   When a positive answer was given, it, too, usually followed a long pause, during which the librarian was apparently considering the matter.

The only ready responses came from those who were obviously unhappy in their jobs and from some who had intended, while in school,

45

to do some other type of work and were now only waiting for such an opportunity. An example of such a response (from a cataloger) was "When I was in library school, I intended to specialize in public services; I'm not using much of what I learned then in this job."

More frequently, responses were of the following nature:

> I had an undergraduate degree in Russian, and I'm not using that.

> Information science was emphasized in library school, and we don't do any of that here.

> I use little of what I learned in the reference courses and the government documents course.

> My job is mostly subprofessional; I wouldn't have needed to go to library school to prepare for it.

The most frequently mentioned preparation that was not used on the present job was preparation in foreign languages, but only a small minority (eight of the fifty-eight) mentioned this.

Since part of the purpose of the study was not only to discover what beginning librarians are asked to do in university libraries but also to determine what these beginning librarians feel about what they are asked to do, each was asked which tasks (assigned as part of his job) he felt were at a full and "proper" professional level and which he felt were at a less than professional level. It was hoped that the answers to these questions would contribute to a better understanding of how librarians define the nature of their profession and what they see as their role, both actually and ideally, in the academic community. The answers, in fact, contributed little to such an understanding, but they supported the hypothesis that librarians do not share a common definition of what is professional in librarianship.

Only thirty-five of the fifty-eight beginning librarians were willing or able to cite specific tasks from those assigned to them that they felt were professional or less than professional in nature. The other twenty-three either avoided answering the questions, stated that they did not have any idea of the meaning of "professional" in this context, or answered in generalities, such as "I consider my job to be a professional one," "My job is about half and half," or "I don't think librarianship can be professional."

The tasks that were named by the thirty-five beginning librarians who gave specific answers are listed below. The number in parentheses indicates the number of librarians who cited that task. When no number appears, the task was cited only once.

TASKS CITED AS PROFESSIONAL TASKS

Book selection (3)
Answering reference questions (2)
Selection aspect of gifts and exchanges
Supervising bibliographic checking of
   block purchases
Original cataloging (6)
Assigning subject headings
Helping people use rare books
Reorganization of archives
Compiling bibliographies
Classifying
Supervision (4)

Decision making
Verifying interlibrary loan requests
   that require knowledge of bibliography
Deciding where to request interlibrary
   loans
Subject analyses (making subject-
   analytic cards for the departmental
   catalog)
Selection and "weeding" of pamphlets
Committee work

TASKS CITED AS LESS THAN PROFESSIONAL TASKS

Typing (12)
Answering "directional" questions (4)
Filing cards (3)
Cataloging books for which the library
   has received Library of Congress
   cataloging copy (2)
Moving books (2)
Indexing school paper (2)
Shelving books (2)
Checking out books and
   pamphlets (2)
Processing gift books
Bibliographic checking of gift books
Checking things in files
Photographing cataloging copy
Descriptive cataloging
Classifying
Claiming serials
Revising completed catalog cards
Making record cards
Checking form of theses

Routine checking of bibliographies
Checking form and spelling of inter-
   library loan requests
Searching the card catalog
Writing letters that answer reference
   questions received by mail
Answering telephone questions about
   whether the library has a certain
   book
Giving tours of the library
Revising everything the clerks have
   done
Sorting the mail
Typing own correspondence
Portrait indexing
Revising periodical records
Typing orders for special materials
Keeping clerical staff payroll records
   and reporting their hours to payroll
   office
Patrolling the building

Perhaps more revealing is the list of tasks that were checked as
regularly performed but were not mentioned in response to these
questions about which professional and which nonprofessional tasks are
assigned.   Table 3 presents information on only those beginning
librarians who were willing to cite specific tasks as less than professional

and on the ten beginning librarians who indicated that no tasks were assigned to their positions that they considered less than professional. The table shows tasks that were checked as performed regularly by these forty-five librarians. Following the task is the number of librarians who checked it as performed regularly, and the second number indicates how many of them mentioned that task as one of the "less than professional" tasks they are assigned.

The only task which as many as half of those performing it regularly thought to cite or considered less than professional was typing. And

TABLE 3 CITATIONS OF NONPROFESSIONAL TASKS BY LIBRARIANS WHO HAD PREVIOUSLY REPORTED PERFORMING THEM REGULARLY (N = 45)

TASK	NUMBER OF LIBRARIANS WHO CHECKED TASK AS PERFORMED REGULARLY	NUMBER OF TIMES TASK WAS CITED BY SAME LIBRARIANS AS LESS THAN PROFESSIONAL
Type letters	9	3
Check lists or catalogs against library's holdings	10	1
Order nonbook materials	6	1
Check order requests to see if the books are already in the library	5	0
Verify bibliographic information for orders	8	1
Maintain book-budget records	1	0
Prepare book orders	5	0
Revise book orders	4	1
Check incoming books against orders	9	2
File cards, etc.	14	3
Revise filing done by others	9	1
Type	19	9
Do descriptive cataloging	14	1
Reconcile L.C. cataloging	12	2
Physically process books (in any way)	18	4
Verify bibliographic information for inter-library loans	3	1
Supervise shelvers	5	0
Prepare information for automatic data processing	2	0

even typing was mentioned by only twelve of the nineteen who had previously checked it as a regular part of their work. On the other tasks listed in the above tables, there was even less agreement.

Most of the beginning librarians, however, seemed to assume an agreement or understanding about what was or was not a professional task. When they were asked to list the professional and nonprofessional tasks assigned to their position, only four of the fifty-eight stated that they did not know the meaning of "professional" in this context or asked the interviewer what he defined as a professional, as opposed to a less than professional, task. No beginning librarian directly indicated the bases upon which he would define a task as professional or nonprofessional. But occasional statements were made that provided indirect clues to the rationale for assigning the tasks to one category or the other.

On the most superficial level, these took the form of negatively defining professional tasks as tasks that are not clerical. Clerical tasks were often cited specifically: typing, filing, looking things up in files, charging out books. These tasks are widely recognized as clerical in libraries just as they are in business offices, and for a few beginning librarians (at least five but probably not more than ten of the fifty-eight interviewed) the conception of professional tasks did not seem to go beyond elimination of these clerical tasks. In other words, they seemed to accept as professional everything that is not building maintenance or that cannot be put in the category of widely recognized clerical tasks.

It should be pointed out, before further description of these definitions of professionalism, that we are describing what beginning librarians said when they discussed the professionalism of their work, not their conceptions about what professionalism ought to be. Often these statements were made in the context of a discussion, without having been carefully considered or thought out, and the investigator believes that inferences can be drawn from them about the *working definitions* of professionalism held by these beginning librarians. If the librarians had been directly asked for their definitions of professionalism in librarianship and had been given time to think about the answer, they would very likely have come up with a fuller, more idealistic, and more satisfactorily "textbook" kind of definition. Such a definition might or might not have pertained to the work these people were actually doing. The definitions that are described here, it is hoped, are close to the ones these librarians *apply* in their day-to-day work. The study attempted to get at these applicable definitions because they are the ones that are tied to job satisfaction and to the effectiveness of the librarian as a professional whose function is to provide the academic community with a service at a professional level.

The next higher-level definition of what constitutes the professional task seemed to be tied to the perceived difficulty of the task. This is, of course, closely related to the simple conception of professional as that which is not clerical, but it would appear to represent somewhat more thought about the matter in that it indicates at least some analysis of what characterizes a clerical task. Several librarians criticized as "subprofessional" tasks which were "easy enough to be done by a good high school graduate," or "routine" (meaning, apparently, frequently repeated and easy to do), or "mechanical and doesn't even require any thought."

This equating of professionalism with difficulty or the demand made upon the performer of the task was, in fact, the implied definition most frequently encountered in the investigation. Fewer than half the librarians made statements from which implied definitions of professional could be inferred, and fourteen of those who made such statements indicated that they were basing the definition on this criterion of the difficulty of the task or on how much demand it makes upon the ability (as distinct from the specialized knowledge) of the person performing it.

Another criterion for defining professionalism that emerged in about half a dozen of the discussions involved the opportunity to make decisions. One librarian, who felt that the work he was doing was at a professional level, expressed his reason for thinking so as follows: "I'm my own boss; in this library you are given a job to do and then left alone to decide how you can best do it." A similar implied definition, expressed by a librarian who felt her work was not at a professional level, was "You aren't given any authority or responsibility around here; I'm told how to do everything I do."

The important variable that emerged in these answers was the difference in practices of supervision employed by different department heads and middle managers. This was the variable that most apparently affected the morale and job satisfaction of the beginning librarians interviewed in this study. In nearly all cases where extreme dissatisfaction emerged, it centered on the authoritarian approach of the immediate supervisor. Complaints of many kinds were frequently heard in the course of the interviewing, but their expression became emotional only in cases that involved supervision that was felt to be too close, too restrictive, or untrusting. The supervisor who could not delegate responsibility and authority was the source of greatest dissatisfaction among the beginning librarians interviewed, and in all cases these dissatisfied beginners indicated that they felt work without the opportunity for exercising decision-making authority and responsibility is not professional work, regardless of how difficult it might be.

The concept of the professional task as one requiring application of a special type or category of knowledge for its satisfactory performance did not often emerge in these discussions. Only two librarians specifically mentioned knowledge of books or subject matter in books as needed for performance of professional tasks in libraries. Only one of the fifty-eight mentioned knowledge of bibliography or the organization of information about books as a basis of library professionalism.

Two other statements were made which implied, in a negative way, that the basis for defining "professional" should be the application of a body of knowledge. One cataloger rejected the idea that a task or position is professional because it requires knowledge of, and ability to apply, a foreign language. As she stated it, "They shouldn't have hired me for this job; they should have hired a clerk who knows [name of language]."

The final statement to be mentioned in relation to this concept of professionalism, deriving from the application of a special body of knowledge, implied acceptance of this definition of professionalism while rejecting it for librarianship: "It seems to me that librarianship can't really be called a profession. I doubt that there is enough of a body of knowledge that is learned in library school." Only this beginning librarian denied that librarianship could be professional.

Perhaps the most interesting question raised by these listings and definitions of tasks, according to whether or not they are professional, concerns the tasks of supervising nonprofessional personnel. This, it should be remembered, was the task most often checked by beginning librarians as a regular part of their jobs. Thirty-four of the fifty-seven librarians indicated that they regularly supervise the work of nonprofessional employees. Yet only four of them mentioned supervising as one of the professional tasks they were asked to perform. (One asked the interviewer whether *he* considered it professional, and none mentioned it as a less than professional task.) Nor did any of the statements made during the interviews shed much light on the conceived status of supervising as a professional or a nonprofessional task. This appears to be an issue that has not been very well thought out in academic libraries.

It is obvious that successful supervision of others is a difficult task that many people are unable or ill fitted to perform. It is much less obvious that opportunity and authority to make decisions about the work of the library is necessarily needed for supervision of the clerical staff. If the persons who are supervised are performing tasks that are routine and simply require the following of established rules, little would seem to be required of the supervisor beyond a thorough knowledge of those rules and the ability to exercise control and at least *some* leadership. Such decisions as would be required in this process would be personnel decisions, that is, decisions about how best to deal with people rather than how to carry out library policy. The former kind of decisions may be difficult to make, but only the latter would seem to be necessarily related to the profession of librarianship.

There is even less reason to think that command of the special body of knowledge of librarianship is needed for most supervising of nonprofessional personnel. As stated above, knowledge of the rules of the library and its policies is clearly needed, but neither the interviews in this study nor anything in his experience leads the investigator to think that either a knowledge of the theories and intellectual bases of librarianship or a knowledge of bibliography or books and their contents is needed to supervise most nonprofessional workers in libraries.

The importance of this question lies in the fact that all of the libraries visited in the study are moving in the direction of having a higher proportion of nonprofessionals on the total staff. This trend will be discussed in greater detail below (in the report of the findings with supervisors and administrators), but it is important to note here that in all these libraries the role of the beginning professional was seen more and more as supervising this increased corps of nonprofessionals. All of which would seem to make very pertinent and timely the question asked by one beginner: "Is supervision professional?"

The interviews, and especially the checklist of tasks that was completed prior to each interview, tended to focus attention too much on tasks and thus to lead to a definition of library professionalism only in terms of tasks. But an attempt was made in the interviews to compensate for this built-in bias by directly asking if there were other (nontask) aspects of the position that the beginning librarian considered less than professional. (The responses to this question revealed a good deal more about what was bothering or irritating the beginners and causing them dissatisfaction than about their conceptions of professionalism in libraries.) Only twenty-six respondents answered in the affirmative, and— again—no widely shared opinions or complaints emerged.

The less than professional conditions, situations, and behavior mentioned by the twenty-six beginning librarians are shown in Table 4, and the number of technical services and public services librarians mentioning each is given. The most frequently mentioned problem is listed first and the other problems follow in descending order of frequency.

TABLE 4 CONDITIONS, SITUATIONS, ATTITUDES, OR BEHAVIOR CITED AS LESS THAN
PROFESSIONAL

LESS THAN PROFESSIONAL CONDITIONS OR SITUATIONS	NUMBER WHO CITED CONDITION		
	TOTAL (N = 26)	TECHNICAL SERVICES (N = 14)	PUBLIC SERVICES (N = 12)
Poor or ineffective personnel organization*	15	9	6
Authoritarian supervision†	11	4	7
Librarian not given control over his time	7	3	4
No released time for self-directed improvement	5	3	2
Less than professional salary levels	5	1	4
Beginning librarians fail to behave as professionals or to make their positions professional	5	3	2

*Responses in this category were usually concerned with the way the library was organized and the work apportioned by supervisors and administrators. The implication was that the position in question was or was not a fully professional position because someone higher in the hierarchy of the library had made or had failed to make it so. Representative statements were:

"They [the department head and administration] haven't yet worked out all the routines of the job so as to get it up to a professional level."

"My job has been organized so that it is truly professional."

† As mentioned previously, the beginning librarians who cited authoritarian supervision from their department heads were the ones who expressed the greatest dissatisfaction with their jobs. Representative statements by these librarians were:

"The head of this department lacks trust and confidence in the young professionals. We are given no authority or opportunity to do anything that is really professional."

"We really have authoritarian and defensive supervision in this department. You can't make any suggestions because everything is taken personally."

Thirty-nine of the fifty-eight beginning librarians cited aspects of their jobs that were less than professional. Some mentioned only one subprofessional feature or task; others mentioned several. A few (this emerged clearly in only three cases) believed there was virtually nothing about their position that was professional. When the thirty-nine who believed there were subprofessional aspects to their jobs were asked to explain or suggest some reasons why this was so, a number of explanations were given, but one stood out clearly as the reason most widely accepted by the beginning librarians (and also by their supervisors, as will be shown later). This reason was that there are not enough clerical personnel on the library staff to get the necessary clerical work done. Time and time again, the young professionals reported "I have to do this [clerical task] because it wouldn't get done otherwise. We don't have anyone else here to do it, and we can't get any more clerical staff assigned to our department—at least not this year."

Explanations by the beginning librarians for the less than professional aspects of their positions are listed in Table 5, and the number of librarians who gave each explanation is shown.

An interesting fact that emerges from Table 5 is that the beginning

TABLE 5   Reasons Cited for the Less than Professional Aspects of the Positions

REASONS	NUMBER OF LIBRARIANS WHO CITED A REASON		
	TOTAL (N = 39)	TECHNICAL SERVICES (N = 20)	PUBLIC SERVICES (N = 19)
Not enough clerical personnel to get the clerical work done	24	10	14
Poor leadership, poor administration, authoritarianism, poor organization	15	7	8
Small size of library operation and impossibility of organizing work into separate categories	7	3	4
Tradition, inertia, past policy	6	1	5
A decision maker in the hierarchy overestimates demands of the work	4	1	3
Difficulty of finding adequate nonprofessional help	4	3	1
Beginning librarian is being trained	3	3	0
Beginning librarian has chosen to do tasks in question	3	1	2
Position is incorrectly classified as a professional position	2	2	0
Supervisor underestimates ability of professionals	2	0	2
Beginning librarian and supervisor disagree over professional goals of library	1	0	1
Librarians have failed to demand professionalism	1	0	1
Librarians haven't been well enough qualified to deserve full professional treatment	1	0	1

librarians rarely saw themselves as in training or internship situations. Only three librarians attributed the nonprofessional aspects of their positions to temporary training situation or programs. If it was necessary for young professionals to be temporarily placed in less than professional positions as part of their preparation for becoming fully professional, they were unaware of that fact. Good arguments can no doubt be made to support the contention that persons emerging from a one- or two-year program of education for librarianship are not yet equipped to fill genuinely professional positions, but if this is the case, it had not been made clear to the beginning librarians interviewed in this study. This may indicate a widespread and very serious misunderstanding between beginning librarians and their supervisors and administrators. A substantial proportion of the supervisors seemed to feel that the first job or at least the first few months of the job, after completion of library school, is a continuation of the training and preparation for the profession.

An interesting though not statistically significant difference emerged between the technical services and public services librarians in their attitudes toward their education and preparation. When asked whether and in what respects their preparation had been less than adequate to meet the needs of their jobs, the beginning librarians responded:

	TOTAL	TECHNICAL SERVICES	PUBLIC SERVICES
Preparation was adequate to meet the needs of my job	27	10	17
Preparation was less than adequate	31	19	12

The technical services librarians who answered this question were apparently less satisfied with the adequacy of their preparation than the public services librarians.

The aspects of inadequacy that were mentioned by the librarians were varied, and no clear pattern emerged. Table 6 shows the inadequacies that were mentioned and lists them in descending order of mention.

The majority of the beginning librarians reported that they had wished and intended, while in library school, to work in a university library:

	TOTAL	TECHNICAL SERVICES	PUBLIC SERVICES
Decided before completing library school that they intended to work in a university library	38	19	19
Did not so decide until they were offered job in a university library	20	10	10

TABLE 6   Reports of Inadequate Preparation

AREAS OF PREPARATION INADEQUATE FOR JOB DEMANDS	TOTAL (N=31)	TECHNICAL SERVICES (N=19)	PUBLIC SERVICES (N=12)
		NUMBER WHO MENTIONED EACH AREA OF INADEQUACY	
Practical work in libraries	7	4	3
Supervision of others	7	6	1
Work with serials	7	5	2
Government publications	5	1	4
Trade, national, and subject bibliographies	4	2	2
Cataloging practice	3	3	0
Knowledge of the literature of a particular subject	3	2	1
Languages	3	2	1
Acquisition techniques	2	2	0
Knowledge of specialized reference materials	2	0	2
Nonbook materials	2	0	2
Foreign bibliography	1	0	1
Library of Congress classification	1	0	1
Planning and organizing techniques	1	1	0

About half of the thirty-eight who reported they had made the decision to work in a university library before completing their professional education remembered having made the decision while in library school and about half remembered having so decided even before they entered library school:

	TOTAL	TECHNICAL SERVICES	PUBLIC SERVICES
Decided while in library school that preference was to work in a university library	17	9	8
Decided before entering library school that preference was to work in a university library	21	10	11

Only a minority, on the other hand, had decided to specialize in a particular type of work or in work with material in a particular subject before they had completed their professional master's degree program:

	TOTAL	TECHNICAL SERVICES	PUBLIC SERVICES
Decided before completing library school to become a subject specialist librarian	17	8	9
Did not intend to become a subject specialist librarian	41	21	20
Decided while in library school to become a subject specialist librarian	4	3	1
Decided before entering library school to become a subject specialist librarian	13	5	8
Decided before completing library school to specialize in the type of library work they were doing at the time of interview	20	5	15
Did not decide until offered job to do present type of library work	38	24	14
Decided while in library school to specialize in present type of work	15	2	13
Decided before entering library school to specialize in present type of work	4	2	2

Despite the fact that thirty-nine beginning librarians felt that their positions failed to achieve full professional stature, most of them reported that they liked being a librarian:

	TOTAL	TECHNICAL SERVICES	PUBLIC SERVICES
Liked being a librarian	35	19	16
Noncommittal	16	7	9
Disliked being a librarian	5	3	2

Of the five who reported that they disliked being a librarian, four indicated that authoritarian supervision by their department heads was the reason for their feeling, and one felt that the work he was doing (cataloging) was incompatible with his personality.

The final question that was asked each of the beginning librarians produced disappointing results. "In what direction do you hope to move in librarianship?" was intended to bring out answers that would reveal what the beginning librarians saw as a professional ideal, or at least what each saw as the professional ideal for himself. The answers, however, failed to bring this out. Most of the beginning librarians did not wish to or could not answer the question. Most indicated that they hadn't planned, or even thought much about what they would do in the future, beyond waiting to see what openings or opportunities presented themselves.

The answers of those who responded to the question are listed below in descending order of frequency:

DIRECTIONS IN WHICH BEGINNING LIBRARIANS INDICATED THEY HOPED TO MOVE IN THE FUTURE	TOTAL	TECHNICAL SERVICES	PUBLIC SERVICES
Intend to continue in same type of work	4	2	2
Not interested in librarianship except as a job to provide added family income	3	3	0
Administration	2	2	0
Acquire several different types of library experience before deciding	2	2	0
Subject specialization	2	2	0
Public library work	1	1	0
Special library work	1	0	1

Reviewing the findings of the completed checklists of tasks and the interviews held with beginning librarians, we see that these beginners were performing a wide variety of tasks, many of which are widely recognized as subprofessional. It is also clear that a majority of the beginning librarians felt their jobs contained significant components at a less than professional level. Evidence did not emerge, however, of a clear definition of "professional." There seems to be a lack of a shared conception of, or even much thought about, the meaning and practical implications of professionalism in a university library. Nor did these beginning librarians indicate that they could see themselves moving toward a more mature sense or performance of a professional role.

In most cases they did not believe they were in a period of extended training or internship; they did not attribute blame for the nonprofessional components of their positions to their lack of readiness or their personal or group failure to assert their professional authority and accept their professional responsibilities; and, finally, they did not foresee and predict growth toward a more nearly professional role in the future.

Chapter 5

Attitudes of supervisors and administrators toward new librarians

The interviews with administrators and supervisors were less informative than those with beginning librarians. The findings, consequently, were less clear and conclusive about some of the issues of concern in the study. Several supervisors showed little patience with questions about professionalism—it was, in fact, a word that many of them seemed to find irritating. The implication of their remarks was that this topic receives more attention in librarianship than it deserves. And yet, in light of this attitude, there is irony in the situation found in the investigation: few librarians seem to share a common conception of just what is being talked about when the term profession is used in regard to librarianship.

The findings about the conceptions held by administrators and supervisors about professionalism, inconclusive as they are, will be discussed in greater detail below, but first let us look at some of the less ambiguous findings.

One of the hypotheses this study intended to test was that most library administrators and supervisors believe that beginning librarians come to their first professional position inadequately prepared to do the jobs that are needed in university libraries. The responses obtained in the interviews of supervisors and administrators did not, however, support this hypothesis. More than half of the respondents said they were satisfied with the preparation and subsequent performance of the beginning librarians they had hired in recent years.

Furthermore, they indicated that their opportunities to obtain well-prepared and well-qualified librarians seem to be improving. The number of applicants is increasing and these applicants are—on average—better educated and better qualified than the applicants of five or ten years ago. Thus, the majority indicated, it is becoming easier to obtain beginning librarians who meet the needs of the positions for which they are hired. Only in technical services did a majority (eleven out of twenty-one) indicate dissatisfaction with the beginners they have hired.

The responses of the supervisors and administrators were as follows:

TYPE OF RESPONSE	ADMINIS-TRATORS (N = 12)	SUPERVISORS (N = 44)	TECHNICAL SERVICES SUPERVISORS (N = 21)	PUBLIC SERVICES SUPERVISORS (N = 23)
Expressed no dissatisfaction	4	14	4	10
Satisfied with beginning librarians they have hired but indicated areas of preparation in which many applicants for positions have been weak	7	12	6	6
Not satisfied with beginning librarians they have recently hired	1	18	11	7

The expressions of dissatisfaction were varied, and no clear pattern or area of widespread dissatisfaction emerged. An important difference between two of the above categories, however, should be emphasized: the responses of the seven administrators and twelve supervisors who were satisfied with the beginning librarians they have hired in recent years were usually quite different from the responses of those supervisors and the one administrator who expressed dissatisfaction. The concerns of the former were much more abstract and theoretical; their approach reflected a desire to move the profession closer to an ideal. It lacked the sense of immediacy and irritation that was often projected in the answers of those who had some present source of dissatisfaction.

(On the following pages the responses expressing dissatisfaction are presented in descending order of the frequency with which they were stated. For each category, typical expressions of supervisors or administrators are quoted. Following the quoted statements are the number of individuals in the different library positions who expressed that type of dissatisfaction.)

The type of dissatisfaction that was most often expressed about beginning librarians, and the most intense and immediate concern, was that beginners showed poor attitudes, professional irresponsibility, or personalities incompatible with the demands of the positions they had accepted. The essential concern was with character traits rather than with ability or education. Typical statements made by administrators and supervisors were:

> Library schools should be more stringent in their selection; especially, they should look more closely at personal characteristics.

> The problem of the one failure we have had in this department recently was clearly a personality problem.

> He could not tolerate the detail needed for cataloging. It was essentially a personality problem.

> When we've had problems, it's been because of attitudes and personality conflicts.

> Where beginning librarians have been inadequate is in personality—laziness.

> People coming out of library school now are not really professionally minded at all. They are jurisdictional minded. They won't pick up a book or put away a catalog drawer. They don't have a service concept. New librarians are not dedicated the way they used to be.

> The deficiencies we have encountered have been in personality and attitudes. The emphasis in library school on professionalism may be aggravating this.

> Personality and personal motivation is usually the problem when a problem occurs.

> The weakness of new librarians has been in their willingness to do things rather than in their training.

The number of administrators and supervisors who expressed dissatisfaction regarding personalities and attitudes of beginning librarians were as follows:

	ADMINIS- TRATORS	SUPERVISORS	TECHNICAL SERVICES SUPERVISORS	PUBLIC SERVICES SUPERVISORS
Number reporting inadequacies in personality and attitude in beginning librarians	2	19	6	13

Not far behind the concern about personality and attitude problems (and perhaps closely related to it) was dissatisfaction with the awareness of beginners regarding librarians' duties in university libraries. Typical expressions of this type of inadequacy were:

> There are a lot of underprepared people as far as university libraries are concerned—people who just don't know what university libraries are all about.

> All too many librarians have mistaken conceptions about what they will be doing during their first two years on the job.

> There should be more in library school about how departments operate, how the work gets done.

> Students in library school often don't know what the work in a library involves. I would like to see a more efficient counseling system to direct students along a path best utilizing their potential.

> The first reaction is often "This job is nothing like what I expected from library school."

> Beginners have no sympathy for the difficulties and complexities involved in a large library situation. They cannot understand the problems and delays and why they occur.

	ADMINIS-TRATORS	SUPERVISORS	TECHNICAL SERVICES SUPERVISORS	PUBLIC SERVICES SUPERVISORS
Number reporting beginning librarians inadequately informed about actual work in libraries	2	15	11	4

The concern with problems of personality and attitude, it should be noted, was most often expressed by supervisors in public services areas. The concern with problems of lack of knowledge about the work of the library (and the consequent danger of taking a job for which one is poorly suited) was most often expressed by supervisors in the technical services departments. Administrators expressed little concern about either problem.

The type of inadequacy in beginners that was the most frequently expressed concern of administrators was inadequacy in subject knowledge. Yet, surprisingly, it was mentioned as a current problem by only four administrators and eight supervisors. It is shown below (in the discussion of the responses to the question about future demands on beginning librarian positions) that several more administrators and supervisors see greater subject specialization as the trend in university libraries, and they anticipate a greater need for librarians with higher degrees in subject specialties, but only a minority expressed a sense of present inadequacy in this respect—such as:

> We now have positions established for collection developers, and these people need more subject knowledge. We have been able to fill these positions with people who have the knowledge—in fact, very good people —but a lot of the applicants coming out of library school wouldn't be qualified.

> Scientific subject knowledge is often not available in catalogers.

> When difficulties [in filling professional positions] have been encountered, it is usually in finding applicants with the right subject specialty.

> Beginning librarians have not been strong enough in specialties, especially sciences.

> The problem is finding a combination of library training and subject preparation. Either, separately, is in plentiful supply.

> Science specialists are hard to find.

The responses were as follows:

	ADMINIS-TRATORS	SUPERVISORS	TECHNICAL SERVICES SUPERVISORS	PUBLIC SERVICES SUPERVISORS
Number reporting beginning librarians have inadequate subject knowledge	4	8	4	4

Beginning librarians frequently expressed a sense of inadequate preparation for supervising the work of others—and it will be remembered that supervision of nonprofessionals was the task most often checked in the beginning librarians' checklist of tasks performed. The administrators and supervisors of beginning librarians, however, did not express much concern over beginning librarians' lack of preparation for supervising. When a sense of inadequacy along this line was expressed, it tended to be quite general or even vague. There was none of the sense of urgency or strong feeling that characterized some of the previously quoted complaints.

Expressions of this type of inadequacy were:

Administrative ability is hard to find among library school graduates.

They lack supervisory ability.

New people generally don't know anything about supervision, and they have to supervise subprofessional staff.

There is a lack of management training in library school.

The number of these responses was as follows:

	ADMINIS-TRATORS	SUPERVISORS	TECHNICAL SERVICES SUPERVISORS	PUBLIC SERVICES SUPERVISORS
Beginning librarians lack ability or preparation for supervising others	2	5	4	1

More practical work experience for beginners, before they come to their first professional position, was another desire expressed by some administrators and supervisors. Typical statements were:

Some kind of internship program carefully related to their studies is needed in library schools.

One of the most important things that should be incorporated into the library school program is some on-the-job training.

Some practical work experience should be required either before or during library school.

Students are not getting any operational knowledge. I would like to see internship work as part of the library school program.

It should be noted, at this point, that almost as many administrators and supervisors made statements that would seem to contradict the desire for more practical work experience in library education. Examples of the opposing points of view were:

What is needed is more theory—more emphasis on why and less on how.

I'm satisfied with the people we've hired in this department. As long as they understand the basic principles, it's easy for us to show them how we do things here.

Library school should provide more theory.

The responses were as follows:

	ADMINIS-TRATORS	SUPERVISORS	TECHNICAL SERVICES SUPERVISORS	PUBLIC SERVICES SUPERVISORS
Number reporting beginning librarians need to have more practical work experience	3	4	1	3

Another dissatisfaction, which was expressed by only seven of the fifty-seven administrators and supervisors, involved the beginners' knowledge of books and bibliography. (This concern was expressed by none of the administrators.) If knowledge of books and bibliography is central to achieving the basic purposes of libraries, and if a major part of the function of top administrators is defining and watching over the basic purposes and how well they are being achieved by the institution as a whole, the adequacy of staff members in such a primary factor could be expected to be of major concern to administrators. The fact that none of them expressed dissatisfaction about beginners' knowledge of books and bibliography is, then, an indication that this is a strong feature of library education, or that the above syllogism is fallacious.

Typical statements by dissatisfied supervisors were:

More stress should be given to bibliography in library school.

I wish beginners had more appreciation of the fine art of bibliography.

Yes, there is an inadequacy in book knowledge—especially a knowledge of bibliography that permits an intelligent approach to a new field.

The number making these responses was as follows:

	ADMINIS-TRATORS	SUPERVISORS	TECHNICAL SERVICES SUPERVISORS	PUBLIC SERVICES SUPERVISORS
Beginning librarians have an inadequate knowledge of books and bibliography	0	7	3	4

The only other dissatisfaction expressed by as much as 10 percent of the administrators and supervisors involved the inherent abilities and intellectual potential of beginners. Typical statements were:

Too often there is not enough potential for growth, not enough intellectual curiosity.

Some just lack general education and intelligence.

The problem we encounter all too often in reference is a deficiency of intellectual curiosity and imagination.

These responses were expressed as follows:

	ADMINIS- TRATORS	SUPERVISORS	TECHNICAL SERVICES SUPERVISORS	PUBLIC SERVICES SUPERVISORS
Beginning librarians lack the needed inherent abilities	2	4	0	4

Several other areas or types of inadequacy in beginning librarians were mentioned by a few administrators or supervisors. These additional sources of dissatisfaction are named and the numbers are mentioned in Table 7.

An interesting finding, which perhaps deserves special attention, was the lack of concern with beginners' knowledge of automation and computers. As shown below, several administrators and supervisors predicted that the computer will be more important in university libraries in the future, but only two administrators (and no supervisors) indicated dissatisfaction with the beginning librarians' knowledge about computers. This would appear to be consistent with the reports of beginners about the work they are doing: on the checklist of tasks performed, only six indicated that they prepare information for automatic data processing (in most cases a clerical task) and only one said that he worked, even occasionally, on systems analyses. Both of these findings would seem to indicate that the computer is not yet playing a significant part in the professional aspects of the work being done in the University of California libraries. Nor do administrators and supervisors feel much immediate concern about a lack of personnel who are prepared to work with the computer. (The interviews with the beginners convinced the investigator that very few of them are so prepared at the present time.)

In the interviews with library administrators, subject specialization was pursued beyond the general questions about satisfaction with beginning librarians. In an attempt to discover broader policy or trends, the administrators were asked whether their library had a place for beginning librarians with subject matter preparation beyond the bachelor's degree, and particularly for beginning librarians with subject Ph.D. degrees. It was apparent from the answers that university-wide policies have not been established and that practices—and even opinions—are only poorly formulated in the individual libraries.

TABLE 7   TYPES OF DISSATISFACTION WITH BEGINNING LIBRARIANS MENTIONED BY LESS THAN 10% OF ADMINISTRATORS AND SUPERVISORS

TYPE OF DISSATISFACTION EXPRESSED	NUMBER EXPRESSING EACH TYPE OF DISSATISFACTION			
	ADMINIS-TRATORS	SUPERVISORS	TECHNICAL SERVICES SUPERVISORS	PUBLIC SERVICES SUPERVISORS
Lack of adequate knowledge of serials	0	5	3	2
Lack of adequate knowledge of the techniques of reference	1	4	0	4
Lack of adequate knowledge of foreign languages	0	5	1	4
Lack of previous opportunities to specialize either by type of library or type of work	2	2	2	0
Lack of adequate knowledge of methodology of research	2	1	0	1
Lack of knowledge in dealing with the business world	1	2	2	0
Lack of knowledge in theory and principles of librarianship	2	1	1	0
Lack of knowledge in cataloging instruction	0	2	2	0
Lack of knowledge about government documents	0	2	0	2
Lack of knowledge about automation and computers	2	0	0	0
Lack of familiarity with Library of Congress classification	0	1	1	0

When they were asked what requirements, if any, their library had for subject matter preparation beyond the bachelor's degree for any of their beginning librarian positions, the answers were as follows:

No such requirements	8
No answer	1
"A master's degree in a subject is given preference when we fill a position now, and I expect it to be a formal require-ment in the future."	1
"We prefer a master's when available."	1
"Our reference-bibliographer positions require subject master and library de-grees." (This was the only answer in-dicating the official establishment of such a requirement.)	1

The situation was made considerably less clear, however, by the responses to the question "If you could find beginning librarians with subject Ph.D.s, would you be able to offer them positions commensurate with their preparation?" Only four of the administrators said no, and only one of those four indicated that he was opposed to the idea of librarians with a subject Ph.D. degree. Six of the twelve administrators felt that the subject Ph.D. has, or in the near future will have, a place in their library, primarily in a book selection or collection development role.

The responses to the question were:

No, we would not be able to offer them positions	4
No answer	2
Yes (now or in the near future)	6

Two of the four who said no went on to say that they would like to be able to hire subject Ph.D.s, or that this appeared to be the trend in university libraries. Some of the statements made by those who responded positively were:

The real potential is there for subject Ph.D.s as subject or language bibliographers.

Yes, as subject bibliographers.

We have two such jobs now; more are planned.

Our intention is to develop a subject specialist reference bibliographer corps. About ten of these would be our goal. The faculty has been very favorable to the idea.

The apparent discrepancy between the answers about formal requirements for subject preparation at about the master's level (only one library reported such a formal requirement) and about openings for holders of Ph.D. degrees (three libraries reported having such positions and two intend to have them in the near future) can be explained, in part, by the fact that several administrators prefer not only librarians with Ph.D.s but experienced librarians, rather than beginners, for those bibliographer positions. They reported that in some cases they have hired library beginners or even Ph.D. holders without a library degree, but this was not their preferred practice, and no beginners currently held the positions.

It is apparent that most of the administrators who anticipate development of a corps of bibliographers with an advanced subject degree see this corps as only a small part of the professional staff of the library. (Already, some librarians resentfully refer to the bibliographers as an aristocratic elite.) There was no indication that any administrators saw the work of the bibliographers as exemplifying what is genuinely professional in librarianship, or that they anticipate that this is the direction in which the profession of librarianship as a whole is moving in university libraries.   Rather, they seem to see the position of the bibliographers as a new position that is being added to the organizational structure.

The function of these bibliographers is to improve the library's performance in book selection, collection building, and, in some cases, high-level reference work. But the present professional positions are not being supplanted by, or upgraded to, these bibliographer positions. Where changes are being made in the present professional positions, the reasons for change and the anticipated direction of change would seem to have little relationship to the fact that there also seems to be a trend toward developing a corps of bibliographers at a high professional level. In short, there is evidence to suggest that the University of California libraries might be moving toward two distinct categories of "professional" positions, the smaller of which (the bibliographers) would more nearly embody the ideal of library professionalism as defined in chapter 2.

This impression that the advanced degree-holding bibliographers are seen as forming only a small and rather independent part of the professional staff of the library was reinforced by the fact that beginning librarians did not see these positions in their own futures. None of the beginning librarians stated that he hoped or intended to become a bibliographer. Nor did any of them indicate that he was advised or encouraged to prepare himself to become a bibliographer. Again, only two of the beginning librarians indicated that they hoped even to work in a position in the library that would involve greater subject specialization.

The beginning librarians' apparent lack of concern with, even awareness of, the appearance and development of the positions of specialist bibliographers is all the more striking when the other areas of change anticipated by administrators and supervisors are examined. Except in this area of greater need for specialization and anticipation of a place (though only a few) for the specialist holding a Ph.D., the expected changes in the near future that were reported by administrators and supervisors were also anticipated by beginning librarians. It was also apparent that some of these other changes are stimulating considerable interest, concern, and often eagerness at all levels of the professional staffs at the eight libraries visited.

The most frequently mentioned change that is occurring, and is expected to continue at least into the near future, is the increase in the ratio of nonprofessional to professional staff. There was considerable agreement at all levels that what is needed is more clerical and library assistant personnel. The administrators and supervisors anticipate adding clerical and library assistant positions, rather than professional positions, whenever they have budget increases for staff during the next few years, and there were even some predictions that the professional staff would be cut and the money reallocated to nonprofessional positions. In several libraries, an organizational structure with a ratio of ten nonprofessionals to one professional was being considered or at least discussed as a serious possibility.

Several other anticipated changes were mentioned in response to the question put to supervisors and administrators about their expectations for the near future. None of the changes, other than an upgrading of professional positions and concurrent lowering of the ratio of professional to nonprofessional positions, was mentioned by more than a minority of the administrators and supervisors. The next most frequent response, in fact, was that no change in beginning librarian positions is expected during the next few years.

The responses to the question are listed in Table 8 in descending order of frequency. For each type of anticipated change, the number of administrators and supervisors of various types of library activity who mentioned that change is indicated.

It became apparent very early in the study that changes were being planned in the work and expected performance of many beginning librarians. A direct question was therefore inserted into the interview

TABLE 8   CHANGES IN PROFESSIONAL POSITIONS ANTICIPATED BY ADMINISTRATORS AND SUPERVISORS

	NUMBER THAT ANTICIPATES EACH TYPE OF CHANGE			
TYPE OF CHANGE EXPECTED	ADMINIS-TRATORS (N=12)	SUPERVISORS (N=45)	TECHNICAL SERVICES SUPERVISORS (N=22)	PUBLIC SERVICES SUPERVISORS (N=23)
There will be a higher ratio of nonprofessionals to professionals in the library, and many of the less than professional tasks now being carried out by professionals will be reassigned to nonprofessional staff. In the process, the professional positions will become more academic and more professionally demanding, but perhaps fewer in number	8	26	15	11
No change expected (or unwilling to make any prediction)	0	17	6	11
Librarians will need more subject specialization	6	10	7	3
Number of positions open to beginners will decrease	11	4	2	2
Librarians will be expected to assume more responsibility for book selection	5	6	3	3
Librarians will need more knowledge of computers and systems analysis	3	8	6	2
Librarians will have more supervisory or administrative responsibilities	2	7	5	2
Librarians will need more language specialization	1	0	0	0
Professional jobs will become one of two types: (1) subject specialist or (2) administrator	0	1	1	0
More knowledge of processes of information transfer will be needed	0	1	0	1
More and better reference service will be demanded of librarians	0	1	0	1
Broader education and more awareness of what is going on in the world will be needed	0	1	0	1
Instruction of students will be a bigger part of the librarian's work	0	1	0	1

schedule for administrators which asked these planners and policymakers what is happening to the number of positions for which, in the future, they will be willing to consider hiring a beginning librarian. The answers were more nearly unanimous than those to any other question in the study. Eleven of the twelve administrators said that the number of positions for which beginners will be hired was being cut. The twelfth administrator did not answer the question.

Three reasons emerged as explanations for this change—and in fact, the number of administrators expressing any one of these reasons was far from unanimous. The reasons follow in direct quotations from different administrators:

1. Fewer new professional positions are now being funded, so we are hiring fewer new people from library schools. You know, we don't have very much turnover of professional staff here. [This was from the administrator of a library that had undergone a very rapid growth in recent years.]
2. Greater demands are being made, and will continue to be made, on librarians, and so we are filling more of our vacancies with experienced people.
3. We are concentrating our funds on clerical and subprofessional help. That is where we have felt the need was greatest. In the process, we have dropped a few professional jobs in some departments.

Closely related to the expectation of an increasing ratio of nonprofessional staff in university libraries is the attitude toward the professional level of the work being done by beginning librarians. A large majority of the beginning librarians, it will be remembered, felt that their positions were less than fully professional. This attitude was shared by many of the administrators and supervisors—not by a majority of those interviewed but by a majority of those who were willing to answer the question. The fact that several did not feel prepared or did not wish to answer this question (about the professional level of the jobs under their supervision) may have meant that they felt it carried an implication of personal criticism. In any case, at least nine of the administrators and supervisors who were not prepared to say that professionals under their supervision were doing less than professional work were willing to predict that nonprofessionals would do a larger share of the work in their departments and libraries.

The responses to the question whether beginning professionals were being asked to do work at a less than professional level were as follows:

TYPE OF RESPONSE	ADMINIS-TRATORS (N = 12)	SUPERVISORS (N = 45)	TECHNICAL SERVICES SUPERVISORS (N = 22)	PUBLIC SERVICES SUPERVISORS (N = 23)
Beginning librarians in my department or library are doing work at a less than professional level	5	20	12	8
No answer	3	9	3	6
Beginners in my department or library are working at a fully professional level	4	16	7	9

Thus if one leaves out of account those who did not answer the question, a majority of administrators and of supervisors in technical services departments agreed with the majority of beginning librarians that the latter were working at a less than professional level. Only in public services departments did a majority of supervisors (a very slim majority) state that the beginners under their supervision were working at a fully professional level.

As was the case with the beginning librarians, several different reasons were advanced to explain why beginners were working at less than fully professional levels. These reasons are paraphrased in Table 9 in descending order of frequency, and the numbers who expressed each type of reason are shown. Again, the most frequently expressed reason was that the nonprofessional staff was too small, and the inadequacy and/or inflexibility of the budget was delaying or blocking the needed addition of nonprofessionals to the staff.

Supervisors, unlike beginners, often expressed the belief that there had to be a training period on the first job following completion of the master's degree in library school. During this period, the supervisors felt, the position of the beginning librarian must include several less than professional aspects and tasks because these are part of the training program. But "program" is perhaps inappropriate in this context because very few departments have a formal program for the orientation or further training of beginning librarians. And there were no formal programs on a library-wide basis, despite the fact that several supervisors and administrators expressed a wish for such a program.

When supervisors talked about the training of beginners, what they had in mind, in most cases, was simply a one-to-one informal teaching process in which the supervisor introduces the beginner to the operations of the department, instructs him in how to do his work, and then

TABLE 9 REASONS FOR BEGINNING PROFESSIONALS WORKING AT LESS THAN FULLY PROFESSIONAL LEVELS

	NUMBER THAT EXPRESSED EACH REASON			
REASON	ADMINIS-TRATORS (N=5)	SUPERVISORS (N=20)	TECHNICAL SERVICES SUPERVISORS (N=12)	PUBLIC SERVICES SUPERVISORS (N=8)
There are not enough nonprofessional staff members to get the nonprofessional work done	2	18	10	8
Professionals need to have practice doing the nonprofessional work so they will be able to train and supervise nonprofessionals	0	3	1	2
The small size of the branch library makes it necessary for professionals to do nonprofessional tasks	0	3	0	3
It is a matter of tradition. Librarians do subprofessional work because they have traditionally done so. [This answer implied sharp criticism of the profession for allowing the situation to continue.]	1	2	2	0
Beginning librarians are not sufficiently educated to be professional	0	2	1	1
Clerical work is part of the training of beginning professionals	0	2	2	0
Organization of the library staff was not adequately planned or carried out by the top administration of the library	0	2	2	0
The librarian is too often a "glorified clerk" who does nonprofessional work by choice	1	1	0	1
Beginning librarians often lack the innate ability required to be a true professional	1	0	0	0
Librarianship has not adequately defined what is professional and what it is not	0	1	1	0
Librarians do not trust nonprofessionals to do many of the more difficult kinds of nonprofessional work	0	1	1	0

observes and checks his work to catch and correct any errors. Thirty of the forty-five supervisors reported that they have an established pattern for this informal training process with beginning librarians. Four reported that they did not feel a need for any training program, even an informal one, and eleven did not answer the question (in most cases because they were too new to their positions to have decided how they would prefer to introduce beginning librarians to new jobs).

For the thirty supervisors who reported that a training period is needed to introduce beginning librarians to positions in their departments, the average times (to the nearest half-month) needed for that training period were reported as follows:

TECHNICAL SERVICES		7.5 months
Acquisition departments	5.0	
Cataloging departments	11.0	
Serials departments	6.5	
PUBLIC SERVICES		7.0 months
Special-subject libraries	9.5	
Special-materials libraries	7.0	
Undergraduate libraries	6.0	
General reference departments	5.0	

It will be remembered that only three beginning librarians cited the fact that they were still being trained as an explanation or reason for being assigned less than professional tasks or for their having to work in a less than professional situation. A majority of supervisors, on the other hand, felt that lengths of time ranging from three months to as long as two years are needed to train library-school graduates before they are ready to assume fully professional positions.

A large part of the discrepancy would appear to stem from the fact that most beginning librarians were unaware that their supervisors considered their first months on the job to be a training period; the training was so informal that it was not recognized as such by the beginners. Furthermore, the beginners usually did not seem to share the belief of the supervisors that a several-month training period following their graduation from library school was needed before they could fill a fully professional position. It is perhaps not surprising that, in the absence of any official pronouncement to the contrary by the profession, beginning librarians feel they are ready to become professionals upon completion of their degree.

Except for this lack of agreement about the need for, or even existence of, a "preprofessional" training period, there was little detectable

difference between the beginning librarians, supervisors, and administrators insofar as the definitions of library professionalism are concerned.
None of the groups made statements showing evidence of a clearly
developed and widely shared definition.

In most of the interviews with administrators and supervisors, no
identifiable definition of professionalism in libraries emerged. Five of
the supervisors stated that they did not know what the term means or
preferred not to use it in relation to libraries. Others indicated,
sometimes directly and sometimes indirectly, that the meaning of
professionalism was too complex to discuss in the time they had
available.

From those who *did* make statements or provide clues to their
conceptions of library professionalism, a set of definitions, quite similar
to those of the beginning librarians, appeared. Twenty-six of the total
fifty-seven made statements from which a definition (or definitions) of
professionalism could be inferred. These definitions, as framed by the
investigator, are listed in Table 10, and the number and percentage of
supervisors and administrators who indicated they hold each definition is
shown. Following some of the paraphrased definitions, statements of
supervisors or administrators are quoted to clarify or amplify the
meanings of library professionalism that were intended.

Professionalism has traditionally been defined in terms of the application of a body of knowledge, and it has been assumed that one of the
principal functions of the professional school is to impart that body of
knowledge. In most professions it would be inconceivable that the
professional function could be carried out successfully without command
of the requisite body of knowledge.

One cannot imagine a physician with only a smattering of knowledge
about human physiology and medicine, or a lawyer who did not know
law. Yet in the interview-discussions of this study, only a small minority
of librarians (either beginners, supervisors, or administrators) referred
to a body of knowledge of librarianship in considering the professionalism of the beginning librarian. Although, as shown above, five
administrators and supervisors specifically mentioned knowledge of
books and/or users of books as necessary, almost as many implicitly
rejected this idea. Four supervisors dismissed the importance of library-
school preparation. Their point of view was succinctly stated by one,
who said "I don't look at library school as being particularly important.
What counts is more the adequacy of the individual than the degree."

TABLE 10 Definitions (with Illustrative Quotations) of Professionalism as Stated or Implied by Administrators and Supervisors

DEFINITIONS OF LIBRARY PROFESSIONALISM AND QUOTATIONS ILLUSTRATING THESE DEFINITIONS	NUMBER WHO INDICATED SUCH A DEFINITION	PERCENTAGE OF TOTAL ($N=26$) WHO EXPRESSED ANY DEFINITION
Tasks are accepted as professional if they have not been widely recognized as clerical "Catalogers here are professional. They do no filing or typing."	2	7.7
Difficult or demanding work is professional work "There has been no problem of subprofessionalism in serials. The problem has been expecting too much. . . . The jobs are really difficult."	3	11.5
The supervision of the work of others in a library is a professional task "In our planned reorganization professionals will be upgraded. More librarians will be supervising units involving clericals and library assistants."*	3	11.5
Work which is not routine is professional work. The implication is that more than a simple application of already established rules is required. Decisions must be made in order to carry out the task successfully "Most routine cataloging, cataloging for which there is copy available, is done by nonprofessionals. Professionals work almost entirely with original materials."	2	7.7
Professionalism in libraries is an orientation to service—a matter of attitude "A pride in the profession and a desire to serve is what counts." "Professionalism is an attitude toward service."	4	15.4

(Continued)

* One administrator rejected this equating of supervisory authority and library professionalism. He indicated that in his library a separate, nonprofessional hierarchy is being established in which nonprofessional library functions will not only be carried out but will be supervised by nonprofessionals. "We have set up a Library Assistant IV position, which is a supervisory nonprofessional position at a high level. The salary level in this position is comparable to a Librarian II position."

TABLE 10—*Continued*

DEFINITIONS OF LIBRARY PROFESSIONALISM AND QUOTATIONS ILLUSTRATING THESE DEFINITIONS	NUMBER WHO INDICATED SUCH A DEFINITION	PERCENTAGE OF TOTAL ($N=26$) WHO EXPRESSED ANY DEFINITION
Professionalism is willingness to accept responsibility for one's performance and development "A real professional will make his job professional regardless of what others say or do. He has ability and a potential for growth; he does his work as he really feels it should be done and is willing to accept the consequences of his mistakes; he has enough commitment to his profession to try to improve both it and himself." "Too many new librarians aren't professional. They just want a nine to five job with clearly established areas of responsibility and with no demands made on them once they leave at five o'clock."	2	7.7
Professionalism in the academic library involves education of students	2	7.7
Professionalism in the academic library involves scholarship	3	11.5
The professional aspects of work in a library involve application of a body of knowledge about books and how they are used "Beginners are usually not sufficiently educated about books and the literatures of various subjects to be able to be library professionals." "Knowing reference books and understanding people—that is what a reference librarian needs to be a professional."	5	19.3

Throughout the interviews with administrators and supervisors there was much greater and more frequent emphasis on the personality, ability, and attitudes of beginners than on any body of knowledge they did or did not possess.

Chapter 6

The California study: summary and conclusions

The study of the beginning librarian in the University of California libraries grew out of a conviction that more information is needed about the roles of beginning professionals in university libraries—about the work those beginners actually do and how their role is perceived by themselves and by those who supervise and administer library operations.

Although the findings reported in the three previous chapters only partially support the hypotheses underlying the investigation, they reveal some interesting and rather striking situations and trends that had not been anticipated. The most solidly substantiated and perhaps most important of these discoveries is that the positions for which beginning librarians (just out of library school) will be hired are decreasing in number in the University of California libraries and that this decrease is expected to continue for at least the next few years. The reasons for this trend and the concomitant changes in the characteristics of the beginning professional's tasks and functions will be reviewed below.

First, however, it would be useful to look once more at the hypotheses the investigation was intended to test. The essential points in the hypotheses are the following:

1. Beginning librarians perform a wide variety of tasks, representing a wide range of difficulty and considerable divergence from what is usually recognized as professional work in libraries.

2. Supervisors in the University of California libraries assign tasks to beginning librarians that are different from what those supervisors feel the beginners ideally should be assigned.

3. The reason for this difference between ideal and practice is attributable to the belief of the supervisors and top administrators that beginning librarians are coming to their jobs inadequately prepared to perform the tasks that, ideally, they should do.

4. An additional reason for the difference between the ideal and the practice is that many library departments are organized in such a way that beginning librarians are required to perform subprofessional tasks in order to keep the necessary "housekeeping work" of the departments up to date. In other words, the nonprofessional staff is not adequate to do the nonprofessional work and professionals, therefore, are put to work on these nonprofessional tasks.

5. Even though most of the professional staff—beginners, supervisors, and administrators—recognize that beginners are assigned many tasks that are less than professional, a widely shared and clear conception of the "proper" or ideal role of the beginning librarian is not found at any level in the university library.

6. This lack of a widely shared conception of the ideal role of the beginning professional is not surprising because there is no clear definition, widely shared by librarians in these university libraries, of what constitutes professionalism and the ideal professional functions of librarianship.

7. Confusion, vague generalizations, and lack of agreement characterize the answers or definitions of librarians at all levels regarding the problems of library professionalism.

The findings of the study clearly support most of these points, but not all of them. The fifty-eight beginning librarians—as indicated by their responses on the checklist of tasks and to questions in the interviews—were performing a wide variety of tasks, from working out a new system for organizing archives to policing the buildings and checking doors and windows to see that they are locked. These tasks range in difficulty from paging books to selecting books for addition to the collection, and many of the tasks (shelving books, filing cards, typing, etc.) have long been recognized as inappropriate and a waste of staff potential when assigned to a professional.

The findings also support the hypothesis that supervisors are often dissatisfied with what they have assigned beginners to do. Twenty supervisors felt that the beginning librarians working under their supervision were assigned tasks that the supervisors considered less than professional. Fewer supervisors—sixteen—claimed that beginners in their departments were assigned tasks at a professional level. Thus, despite the fact that nine of the forty-five supervisors did not answer the question, there is evidence that a majority of supervisors recognize and admit that they assign beginning professionals work that is less than professional.

The next point in the hypothesis is that the recognized difference between an ideal of what beginning professionals should be doing and what in fact they do can be attributed to a belief by supervisors and administrators that beginning librarians come to their libraries inadequately prepared to perform at the ideal level.

This point was not supported by the findings of the study. Thirty-seven supervisors and administrators (65% of those interviewed) expressed satisfaction with the beginning librarians they have hired in recent years. Those who expressed dissatisfaction were more often concerned with the personality, attitudes, willingness, and cooperativeness of beginning librarians than with their abilities or preparation for doing the jobs the supervisors felt they should be doing.

Several supervisors and administrators expressed the opinion that the caliber and qualifications of the beginning librarians they have hired have increased in recent years. Two factors were suggested to explain this improvement. Some felt that library schools are attracting better people to their programs; others attributed the improvement to the fact that more candidates are applying for fewer job openings and, therefore, each library has a larger body of prospective employees from which to choose.

One of the hypotheses suggested that an additional reason for assigning the subprofessional tasks to beginning librarians was the inadequacy of nonprofessional personnel for carrying out these tasks. This, as it turned out, was the reason most frequently advanced for the problem. Beginning librarians, supervisors, and administrators all gave this explanation (involving a shortage of nonprofessional personnel) more often than any other when they were asked why beginning librarians are asked to perform less than professional tasks.

An explanation for why there are not enough nonprofessionals working in these libraries was not clearly brought out. Leaders within the profession, such as Robert Downs, proposed as recently as 1965 that the ratio of professionals to nonprofessionals in university libraries should be about one to two.[1] The almost unanimous opinion of those who were interviewed in this study was that a much lower ratio would be more appropriate.   A ratio as low as one professional to ten nonprofessionals was suggested as desirable by some supervisors and administrators.   There was not enough time to pursue the answers to what had led to the organizational ratio of about one professional to two nonprofessionals.   They are essentially historical, and outside the scope of these interviews, but could be an interesting and perhaps very revealing study in their own right.

The study supports the hypothesis that the library profession, at least as represented by the University of California libraries, lacks a clearly defined and widely shared conception of professionalism and the professional functions of librarianship.   Only a minority of the librarians were willing to make a statement or commit themselves on the meaning of library professionalism as it applies to beginning librarians or to those with varying amounts of experience at various levels in a library hierarchy.

Those who ventured to make a definition and those who made statements containing implied definitions of library professionalism showed little agreement.   The definition that emerged most often in the interviews with beginning librarians was one of the most superficial to come out of the study.   Their underlying point of view seemed to see the professional aspects of library work as consisting of difficult or demanding tasks.   Easy, routine, or mechanical tasks are not "professional"; other tasks, if they are not easy, routine, or mechanical, seem to be accepted as "professional," regardless of what they are.   This was the most frequently stated or implied definition, yet it came from only fourteen of the fifty-eight beginning librarians.

Other definitions had very little support.   Fewer than ten beginning librarians saw professionalism as characterized by granting freedom and authority to determine how one's work can best be carried out and at least have a voice in making decisions about the goals as well as the techniques and scheduling of one's tasks.   The responsibilities of professionalism were not brought up by any of these beginners while they discussed the freedoms and authorities of professionalism.   Only four beginners talked about a body of knowledge of the library profession.

The responses of administrators and supervisors also lend support to the hypothesis that librarians lack a clearly defined and widely shared conception of what professionalism is all about.   The definition that emerged most frequently was that library professionalism consists of those aspects of library work which involve application of a body of knowledge about books and how they are used. But this definition was stated by only five of the fifty-seven administrators and supervisors. Eight other definitions and/or characteristics of library professionalism were proposed or implied by administrators and supervisors, but none of them was advanced by more than four individuals. It is interesting to note that the responsibilities that accompany the prerogatives and authorities of a professional were mentioned by supervisors, but by only two of them.

The hypothesis that there is lack of a widely shared and clear conception of a "proper" or ideal role for the *beginning* librarian in the university library was strongly supported by the findings of the study. Whatever the reasons may be, it was evident that the administrators and supervisors did not share many opinions as to what a beginning professional should or should not be expected to do. Nor was there agreement on how much working experience is needed before a beginner is ready to be a real professional. The beginning librarians, furthermore, did not, in the great majority of cases, seem to realize that any period of work experience following the professional master's degree was expected of them before they could qualify as full professionals.

This disagreement between beginners and supervisors about the readiness of beginners for professional status is, perhaps, the source of most of the ill feeling and resentment that were encountered in the talks with both beginners and supervisors. It seemed self-evident to many supervisors that an inexperienced person, just coming out of a one-year professional education program, is not ready to assume the authority and responsibility of a professional position or to meet the demands that are made by professional library tasks. This seemed not to be self-evident at all to most of the beginners, and they frequently felt that the supervisors were overestimating the weight of the authority and the difficulty and demands of the tasks.

That there is a widespread difference in attitudes between the experienced and the young is, of course, neither surprising nor necessarily regrettable. The traditional roles of the experienced, as guardians of standards and the achievements and accomplishments of the past, and of the young, as challengers of wornout thinking and infusers of new ideas and energies, bode well for the health of any profession. Both are needed, and the interplay between them can lead to growth for all. But what is unfortunate and regrettable in the situations found in the libraries is that these roles and differences in points of view have been so inadequately thought out and communicated. For the young to believe they are ready to shoulder professional authority and responsibilities before the experienced believe they are ready is not a bad situation (if the experienced exercise adequate power to restrain but not to stifle), unless the young are not aware that their elders do not think them ready and—even worse—if the elders do not have a clear idea of what the young should be getting ready for.

These findings raise serious questions about librarianship as a profession. If the situation in the University of California libraries is widespread in the field, can any group who shares so little definition of a profession or so little conception of a professional role justifiably claim that it constitutes a profession?

But the situation in these university libraries is more complex than the above conclusions have implied. The findings also revealed that many, perhaps most, of the librarians interviewed—beginners, supervisors, and administrators—were very much concerned and involved with questions and issues of what tasks librarians are doing and whether professionals or nonprofessionals should be doing those tasks. They are also considering how the work assignment patterns in libraries can be reorganized to upgrade and increase the effectiveness of the professional personnel.

This would seem, at first glance, to contradict the conclusions about the lack of well-thought-out definitions of what is professional in librarianship, but the discrepancy, when looked at more closely, is not real. The impetus for the concern about the work being done by professionals comes not from a real concern about the role that library professionals might and should be playing in our society but, rather, from the pressure of increasing costs and inadequate library budgets. The question that seems, in effect, to be most often asked is "How, in this period of rising costs, can we continue our present level of activities and services without an increased budget?" The implicit answer is "By transferring more of the work an expensive professional staff has been doing to less expensive clerical and library technician positions." The criteria that are applied in this process do not involve the proper functions and goals of the professional but, rather, the difficulty of individual tasks and the amount of training and experience needed to perform them.

In short, if a nonprofessional can probably do it satisfactorily, assign it to that person.

The thought and analysis of library tasks that are involved in this process are, no doubt, desirable and productive. They should lead to more efficient operations, and, if standards are maintained, to more service for the dollars spent. But this thought and analysis are devoted to methods and techniques, not to goals and purposes.

The inadequacies of definition and shared conceptions described above are not being remedied. These are inadequacies in the development of thought about questions basic to librarianship—such questions as: *Why* is there a library profession, What are its purposes in society, What should it attempt to accomplish, In what aspects is it failing to meet its ideals, and What, in fact, are its ideals?

For all the interest and thought that were found by the study regarding the work of professionals, there was very little evidence that much thought is given to these questions. Nor was there evidence that these questions have been satisfactorily answered in the minds of the librarians interviewed. Rather, they seem—all too often—not to have been asked.

A question that naturally arises from any discussion such as this is how these inadequacies might be remedied. How can a more sophisticated conception of professionalism be developed in librarians, and how can they be encouraged to *feel* they are part of a profession? Only by developing such awareness of their profession can librarians internalize its altruistic and service-oriented system of values, and only in this way can they reap the rewards of an enhanced self-image and pride in professional accomplishments. Two distinct needs are stated here. The first is the need for a better understanding of the meaning of professionalism; the second is the need for developing a sense of professional identity.

An intellectual understanding of professionalism, involving both its underlying theory and its application to a particular area of assumed responsibility, can best be imparted by the professional schools in their programs of formal education. Because they can do it most efficiently and effectively, the schools have a responsibility to expend the time and attention needed to ensure that the purposes and meaning of professionalism are clearly understood by all who are about to enter the profession. It must be concluded from the findings of the present study that formal library education has often fallen short of meeting this responsibility.

But it would be unrealistic and unjust to assign too much blame to library schools. Two other factors also should be recognized as probable reasons for the inadequacies of professional awareness found in this study. The first factor is perhaps the more important, and is certainly the more difficult one to deal with. It is the low value society places upon the services offered by librarianship. As long as the clients to be served by a library do not recognize as important and valuable the services they are offered, it is unlikely that the working librarian will be able to develop a genuine sense of professional worth and mission. And without this sense, the librarian feels little stimulus to give serious thought to his professional role.

The second factor, which probably derives from the first, is the weakness of a professional "culture" in librarianship. All too few librarians have developed the sense of community interests and shared purposes that could make their profession a central aspect of their lives and self-concepts. The intellectual understanding of the profession, for which the library schools should assume chief responsibility, is not enough. These *cultural* and *emotional* components are also needed—but there is probably a limit to what formal education can do in providing them. They are, much more, the responsibility of the profession as a whole and all its well-established members, individually. Meeting this responsibility (to the extent that it can be institutionalized) can best be promoted through professional organizations and associations. And again it must be concluded that individual librarians and their professional organizations have also fallen short of meeting this responsibility.

Another interesting facet of this large issue of professionalism should also be mentioned. The academic libraries of California, for some time prior to this study, had been involved in discussion and controversy on the status of the librarian within the academic community. In the university's libraries, this concern resulted in the formation of a number of committees of librarians and some recommendations for changes in the policies of library administration and in the organizational structure of professional positions. One of the most notable documents to come out of these activities, as far as the relationship of the librarian to the library administration is concerned, is the *Report of the Task Force on Academic Library Personnel* of the Berkeley library.[2] This report includes recommendations for (among other things) professional library rankings analogous to faculty rankings, more professional participation in matters of library governance, and professional tenure.

In the discussions and interviews of the study, neither the Task Force report nor other committee activities and recommendations were often mentioned. A few beginning librarians mentioned these concerns with academic status within the university as of personal interest to them, but usually with pessimism as to whether much would come of the committee meetings and reports. Only two beginners cited these activities as one of the causes of changes being made in professional positions in the

University of California libraries. Supervisors and administrators said virtually nothing about these issues. This silence, of course, might be attributable to the sensitive situation at the time the interviews were held, as the librarians might have felt these matters were in negotiation and were not open for discussion outside the negotiation sessions.

Whatever the reasons may be for changes, it was made quite clear by the findings that changes were being made in the libraries of the University of California. Positions were being analyzed and reevaluated to determine whether they involved tasks that could reasonably be expected to be carried out by someone in a lower classification and lower salary level. This means that tasks that had previously been done by professionals were often turned over to nonprofessionals, and more of them will be turned over as the staffs are reorganized to include more nonprofessional positions. The result is an increase in the ratio of nonprofessionals to professionals. And a corollary result is that the number of professional staff positions is not increasing as fast as the size of the library and the total staff. In several libraries the size of the professional staff seemed to be unchanging; in a couple it was declining. In none—not even the small but rapidly growing campuses—was the professional staff of the library increasing in size at the time of the study.

These changes in staffing are, furthermore, causing a significant decrease in the number of positions for which administrators are willing to hire beginning librarians. As professional positions are relieved of many subprofessional tasks that have in the past been assigned to them, they are assigned more tasks of a supervisory nature. And as more of the professional staff take on more supervisory and management responsibility, there is a greater desire to fill the positions with only *experienced* personnel. Supervisory experience is especially valued—particularly if it can provide evidence of success in dealing with and managing people.

The study failed to turn up evidence of much increase in the nonsupervisory aspects of professional positions at that time. This negative finding may very well be the most significant one in the study. As professionals are relieved of nonprofessional duties, their numbers are decreased, at least in proportion to the total staff, and they are devoting more and more of their time to the training and supervision of nonprofessionals, who are doing an ever greater proportion of library work. The findings did not indicate that professionals, after being relieved of nonprofessional tasks, are in any significant way improving or increasing the uniquely professional services that might be offered the university community. Five libraries reported that professionals were working as subject or area bibliographers, but only at the Los Angeles campus has the concept of the librarian as book selector been put into practice (with establishment of a corps of these bibliographers), and even there they form only a small part of the professional staff. Furthermore, they are not expected to increase very much in number, at least not in the near future.

This seems to mean that although the positions of professionals in these university libraries are being upgraded (in the sense that the librarian is being relieved of clerical and routine tasks and is being assigned more challenging and demanding tasks), the changes are essentially mere reorganizations of library operations. The professional is moving to a higher relative position within the library hierarchy; but the librarian is not, except in a few cases, given the opportunity to improve or extend the special services of his profession. The time he gains as a result of being freed from less than professional duties he has to spend primarily on managing and supervising the growing routine operations of the library. Thus the typical librarian does not seem to find much more time to devote to improving book selection. There is even less evidence to suggest that he is finding more time to move into the academic community to discover how the library can better serve that community. And this is perhaps what is needed of the academic librarian, more than anything else, at the present time.

There are reasons to hope for improvements, however. Administrators and supervisors both predicted a greater need in their libraries in the years ahead for subject specialists. This would seem to indicate that if financial problems in universities are alleviated, there may be both incentive and opportunity to increase once more the proportion of the professional staff in order to expand and develop the professional knowledge and professional services which are basic to librarianship.

Chapter 7

Alternative
roles

What alternative roles might the beginning librarian play in the university library? This is one of the most important unanswered questions in the University of California study. Is it possible for a beginner, just out of library school, to be a professional? If not, how might his role be structured to promote his further preparation for professionalism?

The distinctly professional functions of librarianship, as defined in chapter 2, demand a very high level of ability and knowledge so as to provide access to the best recorded information and ideas that will meet the needs of a client and are appropriate to the client's abilities and situation. Accomplishing this purpose in the university setting involves a number of activities that call for an extensive knowledge of subject matter, of books and other information sources, of bibliographic structure and development, and of clients both as members of information-using groups and as individuals with unique sets of needs and abilities. All these types of knowledge must be drawn upon and applied with good judgment by the librarian in arriving at the best solution to each professional problem. Development of high-level effectiveness by the librarian in such demanding problem-solving activities requires a great deal of time, study, and experience.

Even so, it might be that those who arrive at their first professional position with an extensive subject background can best enter immediately into a professional role. The beginner with a subject Ph.D. and a library degree is probably as well prepared to offer service in his area of specialization as the typical beginning assistant professor, fresh from his Ph.D. program, is prepared for teaching. In the process of earning the advanced-subject degree and the professional master's degree, the librarian will have had opportunities to develop his subject knowledge, his bibliographic knowledge, and knowledge of what kinds of information the clients in his field of specialization need and how they typically use this information. In combination, these three kinds of knowledge make up the essential professional body of knowledge of the librarian as librarian, and if they have been mastered, he is ready for substantive professional work. The types of experiential knowledge and skill that this highly educated beginner needs, but still lacks, can probably be developed most quickly and efficiently by entering immediately into the professional role and encountering all its demands in a kind of "baptism by fire."

It would be tempting, and it may be possible under the job market conditions of the 1970s, for universities to select only beginning librarians who have developed a high level of subject expertise and maturity. It would be even more tempting, perhaps, to hire no beginners at all—only experienced and proven librarians. But the error and danger in doing this are obvious. The profession must maintain and renew itself. It must accept responsibility for providing beginners the opportunity to enter and to grow into full professional stature.

It is a fact, furthermore, that at the present time—and probably for some years to come—most beginners come to university libraries without a significant background of work on a subject doctorate. For the nonspecialized beginner, who has a bachelor's (or at most a subject master's) degree combined with a professional library degree, additional study and experience are almost certain to be needed before satisfactory performance as a professional can be achieved. Such a beginner, even after five or more years of higher education (including one or two years of library-school education), is likely to be weak in two aspects of professional knowledge. He will lack (1) sufficient depth in subject knowledge to provide professional information services to advanced students and researchers and (2) familiarity with the information needs and use patterns of such a group of clients.

This beginner, if he is to become professional, needs not only experience to develop those skills and techniques derived from practice but also an opportunity to build his body of professional knowledge and judgment through additional course work, continued study of subject literatures and bibliography, and additional exposure to a university library clientele, which is especially important. This last is the aspect of the professional body of knowledge that has been most neglected by librarianship. In order to build his "client knowledge," the librarian must work closely with clients, not only in providing services but as a colleague, fellow student, and scholar.

Only through such varied contacts can the librarian acquire the understanding he needs of his clients as information users. In the process, he also has an opportunity to win the respect and confidence of the university community.

As a means of clarifying and summarizing some of the issues raised in this work, it would be worthwhile to conclude by suggesting some alternative role models for beginning librarians in university libraries. These are models that either have been observed in actual library practice or are feasible and are based upon some logic related to need and purpose. It was suggested above that the beginner who comes to his first position with a highly developed body of professional knowledge may not need to assume a role structured differently from that of experienced professionals. The role models sketched below are therefore conceived as alternatives for the nonspecialized beginner who has had little opportunity to develop subject knowledge in depth. This person, especially if he is young and just out of the university (without significant work experience), may also lack intellectual or emotional maturity, understanding of people, and other bases for sound professional judgment that can come from a variety of learning and life experiences.

The first alternative model is the traditional role of the beginner who is placed in a hierarchical slot that he seems prepared to fill. This has long been the typical beginning role of the librarian, and if it is no longer so, the change has been very recent. These hierarchical positions to which beginners have traditionally been assigned have almost always been well below what might be defined as a professional level. Most of the work is routine, along with some components of public service desk work or cataloging, and is usually closely supervised.

The important characteristic of this model is that neither beginners nor advanced librarians have seen it as an extension of the preparation for librarianship or as necessarily temporary. Lacking a clear conception of what constitutes professional functions and, correspondingly, of what the library profession should try to accomplish, librarians at all levels of experience have accepted low-level jobs, consisting largely of routine and even clerical work, as "professional" positions.

The beginner's position is usually seen in this model as a testing ground in which he has an opportunity for proving himself and winning promotion to a more demanding position in the hierarchy, such as a department head or branch librarian. But, in the past at least, many librarians who did not prove themselves could remain for years—even a lifetime—in these undemanding, routine jobs. The image of the sour and/or inept librarian is hardly surprising under such circumstances.

A newer and currently popular role model for the nonspecialized beginning librarian might be characterized as that of an "operational trainee." Many (perhaps a third) of the beginners' positions in the University of California libraries would fit this model. Here again, a large part of the job emphasis is on nonprofessional operations, but the important difference is that everyone *sees* the beginner's role as preparatory—and the beginner is being prepared for library supervision and management. Thus the beginner is given a wide variety of experiences in the routine operations of one or more departments so that he will understand them, know in detail how they are carried out, and be able to direct and supervise them.

Beginners in these operational trainee positions often have a professional component in their roles. They might spend some time at public services desks or in professional functions in technical services, but the emphasis usually remains on preparation for future supervisory duties. Nonsupervisory professional functions, such as collection development, developing bibliographical control systems, providing bibliographic access through analysis of subject content, or providing direct aid and guidance to library clients, are not often seen as the major components of their future roles in the library. At least these are not the activities for which their assigned duties are preparing them.

Structured in-service training is a recognized part of the operational trainee role. It has sometimes been called an internship,[1] but for purposes of clarification in this discussion it would be better to distinguish between, on one hand, a professional internship in which the intern is involved primarily in trying out professional activities while receiving some experienced guidance and, on the other hand, an in-service training program primarily involving the learning of procedures and the operational routines of a particular library. The latter would seem to be most effective as preparation for library administration, but the former appears to have very interesting potential for the nonspecialized beginning librarian whose career aspiration is professional work as a librarian.

An internship following completion of a formal professional education program can have several advantages. It makes clear to all that the intern has not yet achieved the necessary qualifications for full professionalism. If well designed, it can provide excellent growth opportunities for the intern. And it can give the profession a chance to observe and assess the professional potential of the intern.

But it must be recognized that an internship is likely to have little value if it does not provide opportunities for professional-level experiences, and this has been the major weakness of many internship programs. If the intern is simply put to work on routine or other low-level tasks, if he is not given the opportunity to meet professional challenges and try new things and make mistakes in the process, the internship will usually turn out to be a waste of talent and potential—or, worse, an exploitation of the intern.

A desirable model for an internship would accomplish two objectives. The intern would be expected to begin making a solid contribution to the professional service and, at the same time, he would be given the opportunity to grow as much as possible in professional stature. Thus his job would necessarily involve professional activities (there would be no need or justification for routine or paraprofessional tasks), but these activities would be planned by the intern in close cooperation with an experienced and successful professional. And the experienced professional would, in the beginning at least, closely monitor the intern's work and help him evaluate his efforts.

The assumption underlying this model is that the professional intern will have sufficient subject and bibliographic knowledge, basic skills in communicating with people, and inherent ability to *begin* performing professional-level tasks—although he still has much to learn. He will probably lack adequate subject knowledge, wide knowledge of the literature with which he is working and its bibliography, and sufficient knowledge of the clients he is attempting to serve. The advantage of the professional internship is that he could more effectively direct his time and efforts in building these types of knowledge if he works closely with an experienced person. In this way the internship could enable both experiential knowledge and formal theory and knowledge of the profession to build from one "generation" to the next.

One of the great advantages of this model is that it permits the intern to move quickly to the level of performance for which his previous education and experience have prepared him. His role, and the temporary limitations imposed upon it, would be determined in large part by the intern himself, acting upon the advice of the experienced professional who is working with him. The role could grow in professional stature to match the intern's growth in professional knowledge and skills.

Whether or not the intern's role is publicly defined as an internship, it would have the advantages for the intern described above. A formal structuring of internships for beginners would have certain advantages to the participating libraries and the library profession as well.

A formal internship would not have to include a commitment for the subsequent employment of the intern. It would give library administrators and professionals an opportunity to evaluate the performance and potential of the intern in considerable depth before making an employment decision.

If the internship were recognized by all as a continuation or extension of education for the profession, it would probably mean lower compensation for the intern than for a professional. If this were so, ethics would dictate a limit to its duration (probably not more than two years) and an obligation on the part of the library to make it a genuine educational and growth experience for the intern. A low-paying internship would also justify "building in" an opportunity for continuing his formal education to enable the intern to further develop his specialized knowledge of subject matter and clientele.

Of the three role models sketched here, all the beginning librarians interviewed in the University of California libraries were performing roles that quite closely match either the first or the second. Few seemed to conceive of these roles as special to their beginning status or as clearly defined and intended to lead to some future professional role. More importantly, even fewer saw the weaknesses of the roles they were performing as suitable preparation for future professional roles. This, of course, could largely be attributed to the fact that none of them seemed to have developed a conception of the role of a genuine professional in librarianship.

But such a conception is now emerging, and it is increasingly exemplified in university libraries in this country. The highly knowledgeable information specialist—with the expertise to provide substantive professional services to all levels of the academic community, working largely independently of the library's operational hierarchy, loyal to his profession, and committed primarily to his clientele—is winning recognition and a place for himself. There is no question that the services offered by this professional are needed, and as the academic community realizes that these services can be obtained, it will come to demand them.

It is now time for the profession to look more closely at the roles it is asking its beginners to play and to decide whether those roles are appropriate and effective in building toward professional librarianship and toward the excellence in library services that our universities need.

Checklist of library tasks

This checklist of library tasks was given to each beginning librarian at least one day before the interview was to be held. He was asked to complete it and bring it with him to the interview.

Please mark each item below with one of the following letters:

R = task performed regularly or frequently
O = task performed occasionally
N = task never or very rarely performed

Do you:

___train subprofessional employees
___supervise work of subprofessional employees
___organize or plan work of others
___participate in library committee meetings
___prepare reports
___dictate letters
___type letters
___read professional literature
___write for professional publication
___attend classes and lectures
___participate in activities of professional organizations
___prepare public relations material

___set up displays
___give tours or lectures
___read book reviews
___investigate needs of library users
___recommend books for acquisition
___check lists or catalogs against library holdings
___look up reviews of books requested by library users
___decide on whether or not to duplicate materials
___consider purchase of materials sent on approval
___decide on acceptability of gifts
___arrange exchanges

___select nonbook materials

___order nonbook materials

___examine material for discard or replacement

___interview salesmen

___check order requests to see if the books are already in the library

___verify bibliographic information for book orders

___search for difficult trade bibliographic information

___maintain book-budget records

___decide where to place book orders

___prepare book orders

___revise book orders

___make final decisions on book selection

___file cards, work slips, or other library materials

___revise filing after it has been done by others

___type

___establish or verify cataloging entries

___do descriptive cataloging

___assign classification numbers or reclassify

___assign subject headings

___reconcile L.C. cataloging

___revise cataloging done by someone else

___physically process books or other materials in any way

___verify bibliographic information for interlibrary loans

___answer reference questions

___help readers use the catalog

___check incoming books against orders

___help readers use reference books

___compile bibliographies for publication

___compile bibliographies for faculty

___work with faculty to help them make better use of library materials in their teaching

___work with faculty on their research projects

___organize and maintain information files

___index

___supervise shelvers

___make decisions about binding

___prepare information for automatic data processing

___develop systems analyses

Other tasks:

Selected library tasks—professional
and nonprofessional

In 1948 the American Library Association published a list with descriptions of activities and duties in libraries.[1] The list divided duties into two categories: professional and nonprofessional. In 1970 a new approach to the categorizing of library tasks was taken by the Illinois Library Task Analysis Project (ILTAP). One of the results of this project was a detailed library task list prepared by Myrl Ricking and Robert Booth and published in 1974.[2] The Ricking and Booth list divides tasks into three categories: professional, technical and clerical.

The chart following compares the terminology and categorizations used in 1948 and in 1974 for listing selected library tasks with those appearing on the checklist of library tasks used in the study of beginning librarians in the University of California libraries.

TASKS FROM THE CHECKLIST COMPLETED BY UNIV. OF CALIFORNIA BEGINNING LIBRARIANS	LISTING AND CATEGORIZATION OF RELATED DUTIES IN THE 1948 ALA LIST		LISTING AND CATEGORIZATION OF RELATED TASKS IN THE 1974 LIST COMPILED FOR THE ILLINOIS LIBRARY TASK ANALYSIS PROJECT BY RICKING AND BOOTH		
	PROFESSIONAL	NONPROFESSIONAL	PROFESSIONAL	TECHNICAL	CLERICAL
Train subprofessional employees	Training and instructing new employees [no differentiation by type of employee]		Multilevel (These functions and tasks are performed in all areas of the library's operation by persons with administrative or supervisory responsibility. They may thus be performed by either professional or technical staff and in some cases even by clerical.) Provides introduction to the work of the unit and on-the-job training as required Evaluates performance on a day-to-day basis and communicates need for and means of improvement		
Supervise work of subprofessional employees	Supervising physical upkeep of catalogs Supervising reserve book collections			Serves as supervisor of major clerical unit Supervises established circulation and registration procedures	

Supervise work of subprofessional employees	Supervising processes for physical up-keep of materials Supervises shelving procedure	Supervises the physical upkeep of catalogs Supervises main-tenance of shelves and files
Investigate needs of library users	Conferring with library users Making and studying surveys of reader interest Investigating community needs	Formulates goals and objectives in conjunction with colleagues and the library's clientele Analyzes user needs and interests to determine future direction of collection Plans, conducts, and evaluates surveys of user needs and interests Consults with representatives of major user groups

TASKS FROM THE CHECKLIST COMPLETED BY UNIV. OF CALIFORNIA BEGINNING LIBRARIANS	LISTING AND CATEGORIZATION OF RELATED DUTIES IN THE 1948 ALA LIST		LISTING AND CATEGORIZATION OF RELATED TASKS IN THE 1974 LIST COMPILED FOR THE ILLINOIS LIBRARY TASK ANALYSIS PROJECT BY RICKING AND BOOTH		
	PROFESSIONAL	NONPROFESSIONAL	PROFESSIONAL	TECHNICAL	CLERICAL
Check lists or catalogs against library holdings Check order requests to see if the books are already in the library		Checking lists with catalog Checking order cards with holdings and outstanding orders		Searches catalog and order files to determine if materials requested are already in collection or on order Checks standard collection-building tools against catalog and notes materials not in collection	
Prepare book orders	Preparing and assembling data for orders	Typing orders to dealers		Assembles data for preparation of orders	Prepares orders for materials
Revise book orders				Checks completed order forms for accuracy	

Make final decisions on book selection	Making final selection for regular orders Preparing lists of material needed	Selects materials Compiles lists of specific materials needed
File cards, work slips, or other library materials	Filing order cards Filing [catalog] cards Shelving and filing	Files order slips and forms Does preliminary filing of cards in catalog Files cards in shelf list and other files Files material by indicated subject heading or classification
Revise filing after it has been done by others	Revising filing	Revises filing of catalog cards performed by clerical staff Makes routine and spot inspections of shelves and files

| TASKS FROM THE CHECKLIST COMPLETED BY UNIV. OF CALIFORNIA BEGINNING LIBRARIANS | LISTING AND CATEGORIZATION OF RELATED DUTIES IN THE 1948 ALA LIST | | LISTING AND CATEGORIZATION OF RELATED TASKS IN THE 1974 LIST COMPILED FOR THE ILLINOIS LIBRARY TASK ANALYSIS PROJECT BY RICKING AND BOOTH | | |
	PROFESSIONAL	NONPROFESSIONAL	PROFESSIONAL	TECHNICAL	CLERICAL
Do descriptive cataloging	Descriptive cataloging	Cataloging fiction	Revises descriptive and fiction cataloging performed by technical staff	Establishes form of author's name — Performs descriptive cataloging of materials for which LC cards or MARC tapes are not available — Catalogs fiction	
Assign classification numbers or reclassify	Classifying Reclassifying		Assigns classification notation using Dewey, Library of Congress, Bliss, or other system, or local expansion or adaptation of one of these systems	Performs simple classification of materials identified in standard tools	

Assign subject headings	Assigning subject headings	Assigns subject headings using standard tools and the library's own authority file	Obtains information necessary to process interlibrary loan requests
Verifying bibliographical data for interlibrary loans	Verify bibliographic information for interlibrary loans	Assists clerical and technical staff with difficult bibliographic searches	Provides clerical staff with needed instructions for processing interlibrary loan requests
Work with faculty to help them make better use of library materials in their teaching	Coordinating the library with the educational program	Informs faculty and students of the personnel, materials and equipment resources available in the library	
	Informing readers about books relating to their special interests	Advises faculty in utilizing the resources of the library in developing curriculum and course work	
	Scheduling and conducting classes in the library	Reviews and makes suggestions on materials lists provided by faculty	

TASKS FROM THE CHECKLIST COMPLETED BY UNIV. OF CALIFORNIA BEGINNING LIBRARIANS	LISTING AND CATEGORIZATION OF RELATED DUTIES IN THE 1948 ALA LIST		LISTING AND CATEGORIZATION OF RELATED TASKS IN THE 1974 LIST COMPILED FOR THE ILLINOIS LIBRARY TASK ANALYSIS PROJECT BY RICKING AND BOOTH		
	PROFESSIONAL	NONPROFESSIONAL	PROFESSIONAL	TECHNICAL	CLERICAL
			Maintains liaison with faculty regarding reserve collection needs		
			Conducts workshops for faculty in use of equipment available in library		
Work with faculty on their research projects*					
Prepare information for automatic data processing				Codes data for electronic processing	Operates keypunch machine
				Writes computer programs following procedures outlined in flow charts	Operates computer input machine

* The concept here was of the librarian as an information resource specialist working as a research partner or member of a research team. Neither the 1948 nor the 1974 task lists included this as an activity for librarians.

Performs desk checks of programs

Tests programs on computer

Conducts studies of library's systems and procedures and makes recommendations regarding them

Recommends on basis of time, cost, and benefit factors whether or not library processes be computerized

Prepares flow charts and diagrams to define systems problems of library procedures

Develop systems analyses

Interview schedules

Administrators

1. Has your library usually been able to hire beginning librarians who meet the needs of the positions open to them?

    If not, is there a pattern to the inadequacies?

2. Do you have a policy requiring subject matter preparation beyond the bachelor's degree for any of your beginning librarian positions?

    How much preparation and for what positions?

3. If you could find beginning librarians with subject Ph.D. degrees, would you be able to offer them jobs commensurate with their preparation?

4. Why is it necessary to have beginning librarians doing nonprofessional work?

5. In what ways, if any, do you expect the demands of the positions open to beginning librarians to change in the next few years?

6. Has your library been cutting down on the number of positions for which you will hire beginners?

7. Do you have any additional statements or comments?

Supervisors

1. How many of the positions in your department could be filled by people just out of library school?

2. How many librarians with less than two years' experience as a professional have worked under you?

3. Are there job descriptions for the positions under your supervision?
   If not, what are the people holding these positions expected to do on the job?
4. Has your department usually been able to get beginning librarians who meet the needs of the positions open to them?
   If not, is there a pattern to the inadequacies?
5. Has it been possible to organize the department in such a way as to make positions fully professional?
6. If not, what are the tasks or aspects of the positions that are less than professional?
   Why do you consider [specific task] less than professional?
7. What are the obstacles in the way of making these positions fully professional?
8. If time is needed for Librarian Is to become fully professional in their positions, how much time would your experience indicate is needed on the average?
9. In what ways, if any, do you expect the demands of beginning professional positions under your supervision to change in the next few years?
10. Do you have any additional statements or comments?

Beginning Librarians

1. How long have you worked here? Was this your first job after library school?
2. What is the official title of your present position and what are the basic tasks assigned to it? (What occupies most of your time on this job?)
3. In what respects, if any, do you feel that your job fails to take advantage of the professional preparation you have had?
4. In what respects, if any, do you feel that your preparation was less than adequate to meet the needs of your job?
5. Which of the tasks you are asked to perform on your present job would you define as less than professional?
   Why do you consider [specific task] less than professional?
6. Are there other aspects of your job that you consider less than professional?
7. Can you suggest why you are being asked to perform less than professional tasks or in a less than professional situation?
8. While you were in library school did you intend to become a university librarian?
   When did you so decide?
   . . . to become a subject-specialist librarian?
   When did you so decide?
   . . . to specialize in your present kind of work?
9. How do you like being a librarian?
10. In what direction do you hope to move in librarianship?
11. Do you have any additional statements or comments?

Notes

Introduction

1. Conrad H. Rawski, "The Interdisciplinarity of Librarianship," in *Toward a Theory of Librarianship: Papers in Honor of Jesse Hauk Shera* (Metuchen, N.J.: Scarecrow, 1973), p.127.

Chapter 1

1. Louis Shores, *Origins of the American College Library, 1638–1800* (New York: Barnes and Noble, 1935), p.140.

2. Ibid., p.146.

3. Ibid., p.157.

4. Kenneth J. Brough, *Scholar's Workshop* (Urbana: Univ. of Illinois Pr., 1953), p.5.

5. Ibid., p.8.

6. Ibid., p.13.

7. Carl M. White, *The Origins of the American Library School* (New York: Scarecrow, 1961), p.63.

8. Harvard University, *Proceedings of the Board of Overseers of Harvard College in Relation to the College Library, 1866–1867* (Boston: George C. Rand & Avery, 1867), p.5.

9. U.S. Bureau of Education, *Public Libraries in the United States of America . . . Special Report* (Washington, D.C.: Govt. Printing Office, 1876).

10. Ibid., pp.509, 516.

11. "Proceedings of the Conference of Librarians at Philadelphia, October 4–6, 1876," *American Library Journal* 1:123 (Nov. 30, 1876).

12. Harvard University, *The Annual Reports of the President and Treasurer of Harvard College, 1878–79* (Cambridge, Mass.: the University, 1879), p.109.

13. Melvil Dewey, "The Profession," *American Library Journal* 1:5-6 (Sept. 30, 1876).

14. Sarah Vann, *Training for Librarianship before 1923* (Chicago: American Library Assn., 1961), pp.26–27, 35–36. Vann, writing about Dewey's presentation of his proposal for a library school to the Buffalo conference of the American Library Association in 1883, tells us that "at the end of the Conference, it was evident that Dewey's plan had not received the unanimous approval of the Association and that no subject proposed before 1883 has created a more controversial and divisive atmosphere within the Association than had the plan for a School of Library Economy."

15. Ibid., p.31.

16. Melvil Dewey, "Library Employment vs. the Library Profession," *Library Notes* 1:50–51 (June 1886).

17. White, *Origins of the American Library School*, p.85.

18. Vann, *Training for Librarianship*, pp.44, 61.

19. University of Chicago Graduate Library School, Twenty-sixth Annual Conference, June 21–23, 1961, *Seven Questions about the Profession of Librarianship* (Chicago: Univ. of Chicago Pr., 1961), p.33.

20. Vann, *Training for Librarianship*, p.191.

21. Charles C. Williamson, *Training for Library Service: A Report Prepared for the Carnegie Corporation of New York* (New York: Updike, 1923), p.9.

22. Louis R. Wilson, "Historical Development of Education for Librarianship in the United States," in University of Chicago Graduate Library School, Thirteenth Annual Conference, 1948, *Education for Librarianship*, ed. Bernard Berelson (Chicago: American Library Assn., 1949), p.48.

23. Susan Grey Akers, "The Relation of the Professional and Clerical Division of Cataloging Activities to Cataloging Courses," *Library Quarterly* 5:101–36 (Jan. 1935).

24. California Library Assn., Library Standards Committee, "Library Tasks: A Classified List," *California Library Association* 3:21–27 (Sept. 1941).

25. Ibid., p.21.

26. American Library Association, Board on Personnel Administration, Subcommittee on Analysis of Library Duties, *Descriptive List of Professional and Non-Professional Duties in Libraries* (Chicago: American Library Assn., 1948).

27. Myrl Ricking and Robert E. Booth, *Personnel Utilization in Libraries: A Systems Approach* (Chicago: American Library Assn. in cooperation with Illinois State Library, 1974).

28. American Library Association, Board on Personnel Administration, *Classification and Pay Plans for Libraries in Institutions of Higher Education* (Chicago: American Library Assn., 1943), 3 vols.

29. Ibid., 3:31, 46, 60.

30. University of Chicago Graduate Library School, Library Institute, Aug. 27–Sept. 1, 1945, *Personnel Administration in Libraries*, ed. Lowell Martin (Chicago: Univ. of Chicago Pr., 1946), pp.2–3.

31. Ibid., pp.4–5.

32. Edwin E. Williams, "Who Does What: Unprofessional Personnel Policies," *College and Research Libraries* 6:301 (Sept. 1945).

33. J. Periam Danton, "Plea for a Philosophy of Librarianship," *Library Quarterly* 4:527–51 (Oct. 1934).

34. Williams, "Who Does What," p.306.

35. Louis R. Wilson and Maurice F. Tauber, *The University Library* (Chicago: Univ. of Chicago Pr., 1945), pp.231–32.

36. Williams, "Who Does What," p.306.

37. Ibid., pp.302–3.

38. J. Periam Danton, *Education for Librarianship: Criticisms, Dilemmas, and Proposals* (New York: Columbia Univ. School of Library Service, 1946), pp. 6–8.

39. J. Periam Danton, *Education for Librarianship,* UNESCO Public Library Manuals, vol. 1 (Paris: UNESCO, 1949), p.97.

40. Ibid., p.16.

41. Ibid., pp.16, 20–21.

42. Saul Herner and M. K. Heatwole, *The Establishment of Staff Requirements in a Small Research Library,* ACRL Monographs, no. 3 (Chicago: Assn. of College and Research Libraries, 1952).

43. Ibid., pp.6–7.

44. Ibid., p.10.

Chapter 2

1. Robert D. Leigh, *The Public Library in the United States* (New York: Columbia Univ. Pr., 1950), p.187.

2. Ibid., p.192.

3. Harold Lancour, "If Librarianship Is a Learned Profession . . . ," *Library Journal* 76:1074–75 (July 1951).

4. Ibid., p.1076.

5. Pierce Butler, "Librarianship as a Profession," *Library Quarterly* 21: 245–47 (Oct. 1951).

6. University of Chicago Graduate Library School, Twenty-sixth Annual Conference, June 21–23, 1961, *Seven Questions about the Profession of Librarianship* (Chicago: Univ. of Chicago Pr., 1961), pp.13–17.

7. Dale Eugene Shaffer, *The Maturity of Librarianship as a Profession* (Metuchen, N.J., Scarecrow, 1968), p.166.

8. Ibid., p.65.

9. Mary Lee Bundy and Paul Wasserman, "Professionalism Reconsidered," *College and Research Libraries* 29:25 (Jan. 1968).

10. Howard M. Vollmer and Donald L. Mills, eds., *Professionalization* (Englewood Cliffs, N.J.: Prentice-Hall, 1966), p.vii.

11. Ernest Greenwood, "Attributes of a Profession," *Social Work* 2:46–47 (July 1957).

12. Abraham Flexner, "Is Social Work a Profession?" in *Proceedings of the National Conference of Charities and Corrections* (Chicago: the Conference, 1915), p.579.

13. Everett C. Hughes, *Men and Their Work* (Glencoe, Ill.: Free Press, 1958), pp.116–17.

14. Greenwood, "Attributes of a Profession," pp.47–49; Howard S. Becker, "The Nature of a Profession," *Education for the Professions,* Sixty-first Yearbook of the National Society for the Study of Education, pt.2 (Chicago: the Society, 1962), pp.35–36.

15. Bernard Barber, "Some Problems in the Sociology of the Professions," *Daedalus,* 92:672–73 (Fall 1963); Greenwood, "Attributes of a Profession," pp. 47–51.

16. Becker, "Nature of a Profession," p.36.

17. William J. Goode, "Community within a Community: The Professions," *American Sociological Review,* 22:194–200 (Apr. 1957); Talcott Parsons, *Essays in Sociological Theory* (New York: Free Press, 1949), pp.43–45; Flexner, "Is Social Work a Profession?" p.580.

18. Lancour, "If Librarianship Is a Learned Profession . . . , " pp.1074–75.

19. "Manpower—the Big Show," *Library Journal,* 90:2713–19 (Aug. 1967); "San Francisco Conference," *ALA Bulletin* 61:820–66 (July–Aug. 1967).

20. "Library Education and Manpower," *American Libraries* 1:341–44 (Apr. 1970).

21. University of Chicago Graduate Library School, Twenty-sixth Annual Conference, *Seven Questions,* pp.71–81.

22. Margit Kraft, "What Would You Do with Brighter People?" *Journal of Education for Librarianship* 7:21–28 (Summer 1966).

23. Eldred Smith, "Do Libraries Need Managers?" *Library Journal* 94:502–6 (Feb. 1, 1969); idem, "Academic Status for College and University Librarians—Problems and Prospects," *College and Research Libraries* 31:7–13 (Jan. 1970).

24. Smith, "Academic Status," p.10.

25. David Wilder, "Management Attitudes; Team Relationships," *Library Journal* 94:498–502 (Feb. 1, 1969); David E. Kaser, "Modernizing the University Library Structure," *College and Research Libraries* 31:227–31 (July 1970).

26. Lewis C. Branscomb, ed., *The Case for Faculty Status for Academic Librarians* (Chicago: American Library Assn., 1970), p.122.

27. Neal Harlow, "Designs on the Curriculum," in Herbert Goldhor, ed., *Education for Librarianship: The Design of the Curriculum of Library Schools* (Urbana: Univ. of Illinois Graduate School of Library Science, 1971), p.11.

28. G. Edward Evans, "Training for Academic Librarianship: Past, Present and Future," in *Education for Librarianship,* p.172. Evans was quoting Eldred Smith, "Academic Status for College and University Librarians," p.11.

29. Paul Wasserman, *The New Librarianship, a Challenge for Change* (New York: Bowker, 1972), p.232.

Chapter 3

1. American Library Association, Board on Personnel Administration, Subcommittee on Analysis of Library Duties, *Descriptive List of Professional and Non-Professional Duties in Libraries* (Chicago: American Library Assn., 1948).

Chapter 6

1. Robert B. Downs and R. F. Delzell, "Professional Duties in University Libraries," *College and Research Libraries* 26:30–40 (Jan. 1965).

2. Task Force on Academic Library Personnel, "Report" mimeographed (Berkeley: Univ. of California General Library, 1969).

Chapter 7

1. For examples of programs that were called internships but might more appropriately have been labeled in-service training, see David J. Netz and Don E. Wood, "The Human Element: A Retrospective Evaluation of the OSUL Internship Program," *American Libraries* 1:253–54 (Mar. 1970), and Vern M. Pings and Gwendolyn S. Cruzat, "An Assessment of a Post-Masters Internship in Biomedical Librarianship," *Journal of Education for Librarianship* 12:3–19 (Summer, 1971).

Appendix B

1. American Library Association, Board on Personnel Administration, Subcommittee on Analysis of Library Duties, *Descriptive List of Professional and Non-Professional Duties in Libraries* (Chicago: American Library Assn., 1948), pp.1–8.

2. Myrl Ricking and Robert E. Booth, *Personnel Utilization in Libraries: A Systems Approach* (Chicago: American Library Assn. in cooperation with Illinois State Library, 1974).

Bibliography

Akers, Susan Grey. "The Relation of the Professional and Clerical Division of Cataloging Activities to Cataloging Courses." *Library Quarterly* 5:101–36 (Jan. 1935).

American Library Association. Board on Personnel Administration. *Classification and Pay Plans for Libraries in Institutions of Higher Education.* Vol. 3: *Universities.* Chicago: American Library Assn., 1943.

————. 2d ed. Chicago: American Library Assn., 1947.

————. *Personnel Administration for Libraries: A Bibliographical Essay.* Chicago: American Library Assn., 1953.

————. *Position Classification and Salary Administration in Libraries.* Chicago: American Library Assn., 1951.

————. Board on Personnel Administration. Subcommittee on Analysis of Library Duties. *Descriptive List of Professional and Non-Professional Duties in Libraries.* Chicago: American Library Assn., 1948.

————. Subcommittee on Personnel Organization and Procedure. *Personnel Organization and Procedure: A Manual Suggested for Use in College and University Libraries.* Chicago: American Library Assn., 1952.

————. 2d ed. Chicago: American Library Assn., 1968.

Barber, Bernard. "Some Problems in the Sociology of the Professions." *Daedalus* 92:672–73 (Fall 1963).

Bartolini, R. Paul. "The Position-Classification Plan for University Libraries." *College and Research Libraries* 9:343–46 (Oct. 1948).

Becker, Howard S. "The Nature of a Profession." In *Education for the Professions.* National Society for the Study of Education, *Sixty-first Yearbook.* Pt. 2, pp.27–46. Chicago: the Society, 1962.

Bolino, August C. "Trends in Library Manpower." *Wilson Library Bulletin,* 43:269 (Nov. 1968).

Branscomb, Lewis C., ed. *The Case for Faculty Status for Academic Librarians.* ACRL Monograph, no. 33. Chicago: American Library Assn., 1970.

Brough, Kenneth J. *Scholar's Workshop.* Urbana: Univ. of Illinois Pr., 1953.

Bryant, Douglas W., and Kaiser, Boynton S. "A University Library Position Classification and Compensation Plan." *Library Quarterly* 17:1–17 (Jan. 1947).

Bundy, Mary Lee, and Wasserman, Paul. "Professionalism Reconsidered." *College and Research Libraries* 29:5–26 (Jan. 1968).

Butler, Pierce. "Librarianship as a Profession." *Library Quarterly* 21:235–47 (Oct. 1951).

California Library Association. Library Standards Committee. "Library Tasks: A Classified List." *California Library Association Bulletin* 3:21–27 (Sept. 1941).

Carlson, William H. "The Junior Librarian and the Administrator." *Journal of Education for Librarianship,* 3:227–35 (Winter 1963).

Danton, J. Periam. *Book Selection and Collections: A Comparison of German and American University Libraries.* New York: Columbia Univ. Pr., 1963.

––––––. *Education for Librarianship.* Paris: UNESCO, 1949.

––––––. *Education for Librarianship: Criticisms, Dilemmas, and Proposals.* New York: Columbia Univ. School of Library Service, 1946.

––––––. "Plea for a Philosophy of Librarianship." *Library Quarterly* 4:527–51 (Oct. 1934).

"Death of the Manpower Shortage." *Library Journal,* 95:3735–44 (Nov. 1, 1970).

Dewey, Melvil. "Library Employment vs. the Library Profession." *Library Notes* 1:50–51 (June 1886).

––––––. "The Profession." *American Library Journal* 1:5-6 (Sept. 30, 1876).

Downs, Robert B., and Delzell, Robert F. "Professional Duties in University Libraries." *College and Research Libraries* 26:30–40 (Jan. 1965).

Education for Librarianship: The Design of the Curriculum of Library Schools. Ed. Herbert Goldhor. Urbana: Univ. of Illinois Graduate School of Library Science, 1971.

Flexner, Abraham. "Is Social Work a Profession?" In *Proceedings of the National Conference of Charities and Corrections.* Chicago: the Conference, 1915.

Gilman, Elizabeth R. "Science Librarians Wanted." *Library Journal,* 76:1854–59 (Nov. 15, 1951).

Goode, William J. "Community within a Community: The Professions." *American Sociological Review,* 22:194–200 (Apr. 1957).

Greenwood, Ernest. "Attributes of a Profession." *Social Work* 2:46-47 (July 1957).

Hall, Anna C. *An Analysis of Certain Professional Library Occupations in*

Relation to Formal Educational Objectives. Final Report. Washington, D.C.: U.S. Office of Education, 1968.

Harlow, Neal. "Designs on the Curriculum." In Herbert Goldhor, ed., *Education for Librarianship: The Design of the Curriculum of Library Schools.* Urbana: Univ. of Illinois Graduate School of Library Science, 1971.

Harvard University. *The Annual Reports of the President and Treasurer of Harvard College, 1878-79.* Cambridge, Mass.: the University, 1879.

_____. *Proceedings of the Board of Overseers of Harvard College in Relation to the College Library, 1866-1867.* Boston: George C. Rand and Avery, 1867.

Hay, Edward N. "Any Job Can Be Measured by Its 'Know, Think, Do' Elements." *Personnel Journal* 36:403-6 (Apr. 1958).

Hay, Edward N., and Purves, Dale. "The Profile Method of High-Level Job Evaluation." *Personnel* 28:162-70 (Sept. 1951).

Herner, Saul, and Heatwole, M. K. *The Establishment of Staff Requirements in a Small Research Library.* ACRL Monograph, no. 3. Chicago: Assn. of College and Research Libraries, 1952.

Hughes, Everett C. *Men and Their Work.* Glencoe, Ill.: Free Press, 1958.

Josey, E. J., and Blake, Fay M. "Educating the Academic Librarian." *Library Journal,* 95:125-30 (Jan. 15, 1970).

Kaser, David E. "Modernizing the University Library Structure." *College and Research Libraries* 31:227-31 (July 1970).

Kraft, Margit. "What Would You Do with Brighter People?" *Journal of Education for Librarianship* 7:21-28 (Summer 1966).

Lancour, Harold. "If Librarianship Is a Learned Profession . . . " *Library Journal* 76:1074-76 (July 1951).

Leigh, Robert D., ed. *Major Problems in the Education of Librarians.* New York: Columbia Univ. Pr., 1954.

_____. *The Public Library in the United States.* New York: Columbia Univ. Pr., 1950.

The Library Association (London). Membership Committee. *Professional and Non-professional Duties in Libraries.* London: Library Assn., 1962.

"Library Education and Manpower." *American Libraries* 1:341-44 (Apr. 1970).

Lyle, Guy R. *The Librarian Speaking: Interviews with University Librarians.* Athens, Ga.: Univ. of Georgia Pr., 1970.

"Manpower—the Big Show." *Library Journal,* 92:2713-19 (Aug. 1967).

Moriarty, John H. "Academic in Deed." *College and Research Libraries,* 31: 14-17 (Jan. 1970).

Netz, David J., and Wood, Don E. "The Human Element: A Retrospective Evaluation of the OSUL [Ohio State University Libraries] Internship Program." *American Libraries* 1:253-54 (Mar. 1970).

Nimer, Gilda. "Professions and Professionalism: A Bibliographic Overview." University of Maryland School of Library and Information Sciences. *Newsletter of the Manpower Research Project* (July 1968).

Parsons, Talcott. *Essays in Sociological Theory.* New York: Free Press, 1949.

Pings, Vern M., and Cruzat, Gwendolyn S. "An Assessment of a Post-Masters Internship in Biomedical Librarianship." *Journal of Education for Librarianship* 12:3–19 (Summer 1971).

"Proceedings of the Conference of Librarians at Philadelphia, October 4–6, 1876." *American Library Journal* 1:45–156 (Nov. 30, 1876).

Rawski, Conrad H. "The Interdisciplinarity of Librarianship." In *Toward a Theory of Librarianship: Paper in Honor of Jesse Hauk Shera.* Metuchen, N.J.: Scarecrow, 1973.

Reece, Ernest J. *The Task and Training of Librarians.* New York: King's Crown, 1949.

Ricking, Myrl, and Booth, Robert E., *Personnel Utilization in Libraries: A Systems Approach.* Chicago: American Library Assn. in cooperation with Illinois State Library, 1974.

Rothenberg, Leslie Beth, et al. "A Job-Task Index for Evaluating Professional Utilization in Libraries." *Library Quarterly,* 41:320–28 (Oct. 1971).

"San Francisco Conference." *ALA Bulletin* 61:820–66 (July–Aug. 1967)

Schiller, Anita R. *Characteristics of Professional Personnel in College and University Libraries.* Springfield: Illinois State Library, 1969.

Schur, H., and Saunders, W. L. *Education and Training for Scientific and Technological Library and Information Work.* London: Her Majesty's Stationery Office, 1968.

"Service and Learning through Internships." *Wisconsin Library Bulletin,* 65:441–45 (Nov.–Dec. 1969).

Shaffer, Dale Eugene. *The Maturity of Librarianship as a Profession.* Metuchen, N.J.: Scarecrow, 1968.

Shera, Jesse Hauk. *The Foundations of Education for Librarianship.* New York: Becker and Hayes, 1972.

Shores, Louis. *Origins of the American College Library, 1638–1800.* New York: Barnes and Noble, 1935.

Smith, Eldred. "Academic Status for College and University Librarians—Problems and Prospects." *College and Research Libraries,* 31:7–13 (Jan. 1970).

———. "Do Libraries Need Managers?" *Library Journal* 114:502–6 (Feb. 1, 1969).

Spence, P. H. "Comparative Study of University Library Organizational Structure." Unpublished Ph.D. dissertation, Univ. of Illinois, 1969.

Stanford, Edward B. "Supervision in Libraries: What It Is—and What It Takes!" *American Library Association Bulletin,* 44:119–21 (Apr. 1950).

"Statement on Faculty Status of College and University Librarians." *College and Research Libraries News,* 35:26 (Feb. 1974).

Stone, Elizabeth W. *Factors Relating to the Professional Development of Librarians.* Metuchen, N.J.: Scarecrow, 1969.

———. "Quest for Expertise: A Librarian's Responsibility." *College and Research Libraries,* 32:432–41 (Nov. 1971).

Task Force on Academic Library Personnel. "Report, November 12, 1969." Mimeographed. Berkeley: Univ. of California Library, 1969.

Tompkins, Marjorie M. "Classification Evaluation of Professional Librarian Positions in the University of Michigan Library." *College and Research Libraries,* 27:175–84 (May 1966).

Toward a Theory of Librarianship: Papers in Honor of Jesse Hauk Shera. Ed. Conrad H. Rawski. Metuchen, N.J.: Scarecrow, 1973.

U.S. Bureau of Education. *Public Libraries in the United States of America . . . Special Report.* Washington, D.C.: Govt. Printing Office, 1876.

U.S. Civil Service Commission. *Guide for the Classification of Positions Providing Professional-level Library and Information Services.* Washington, D.C.: Govt. Printing Office, 1966.

University of Chicago. Graduate Library School. Library Institute, Aug. 27–Sept. 1, 1945. *Personnel Administration in Libraries.* Ed. Lowell Martin. Chicago: Univ. of Chicago Pr., 1946.

―――. Thirteenth Annual Conference, 1948. *Education for Librarianship.* Ed. Bernard Berelson. Chicago: American Library Assn., 1949.

―――. Twenty-sixth Annual Conference, June 21–23, 1961. *Seven Questions about the Profession of Librarianship.* Chicago: Univ. of Chicago Pr., 1961.

Vann, Sarah K. *Training for Librarianship before 1923.* Chicago: American Library Assn., 1961.

Vollmer, Howard M., and Mills, Donald L., eds. *Professionalization.* Englewood Cliffs, N.J.: Prentice-Hall, 1966.

Voorhies, Darrell H. "Job Analysis Is Organization's Tool." *Library Journal* 72:1737 + (Dec. 15, 1947) and 73:33–35 (Jan. 1, 1948).

Wasserman, Paul. *The New Librarianship, a Challenge for Change.* New York: Bowker, 1972.

―――― and Bundy, Mary Lee. *A Program of Research into the Identification of Manpower Requirements, the Educational Preparation and the Utilization of Manpower in the Library and Information Professions.* College Park: Univ. of Maryland School of Library and Information Services, 1969.

Weinbrecht, Ruby Y. "The Junior Librarian." *Journal of Education for Librarianship,* 3:213–26 (Winter 1963).

White, Carl M. *The Origins of the American Library School.* New York: Scarecrow, 1961.

Wight, Edward A. "In-Service Training of Professional Librarians in College and University Libraries." *College and Research Libraries* 10:103–7 (Apr. 1949).

Wilder, David. "Management Attitudes; Team Relationships." *Library Journal* 94:498–502 (Feb. 1, 1969).

Williams, Edwin E. "Who Does What: Unprofessional Personnel Policies." *College and Research Libraries* 6:301–10 (Sept. 1945).

Williamson, Charles C. *Training for Library Service: A Report Prepared for the Carnegie Corporation of New York.* New York: Updike, 1923.

Wilson, Louis R. "The American Library School Today." *Library Quarterly,* 7:211–45 (Apr. 1937).

──────. "Historical Development of Education for Librarianship in the United States." In University of Chicago Graduate Library School, Thirteenth Annual Conference, 1948, *Education for Librarianship.* Ed. Bernard Berelson. Chicago: American Library Assn., 1949.

Wilson, Louis R., and Tauber, Maurice F. *The University Library: Its Organization, Administration and Functions.* Chicago: Univ. of Chicago Pr., 1945.

──────. ────── 2d ed. New York: Columbia Univ. Pr., 1956.